# ELLIDA

## A NEW TRANSLATION BY MAY-BRIT AKERHOLT OF HENRIK IBSEN'S *THE LADY FROM THE SEA*

Currency Press,
Sydney

LA MAMA

CURRENT THEATRE SERIES

First published in 2018
by Currency Press Pty Ltd,
PO Box 2287, Strawberry Hills, NSW, 2012, Australia
enquiries@currency.com.au
www.currency.com.au

in association with La Mama Theatre, Melbourne

Typeset by Currency Press.
Cover photograph by Laurence Strangio.
Image adjustment by Felix Strangio.

Currency Press acknowledges the Traditional Owners of the Country on which
we live and work. We pay our respects to all Aboriginal and Torres Strait
Islander Elders, past and present.

A catalogue record for this
book is available from the
NATIONAL
LIBRARY    National Library of Australia
OF AUSTRALIA

# Contents

*Theatre Program at the end of the playtext*

# 'In my next work, the sea shall play a role'[1]

May-Brit Akerholt

Henrik Johan Ibsen (1828–1906) published his first play, *Catiline*, in 1850. Then followed a career as an artistic director, a journalist and a playwright which saw him becoming one of the world's most performed playwrights, then and now.

By the time of *Ellida* (*The Lady from the Sea,* 1888), Ibsen had written a long series of successful plays, most of which were quickly translated into a variety of languages. Plays such as *Pillars of Society, A Doll's House, Ghosts, The Wild Duck* and *Hedda Gabler* enraged and thrilled, provoked, puzzled and pleased audiences everywhere they were performed. They caused an uproar for two main reasons: firstly, because they exposed the narrow-minded, bigoted prejudices of contemporary society, including family relationships—time was not yet ripe for the kind of feminism the plays forced them to confront. Secondly, their disregard for conventional dramatic traditions challenged society's long-standing and comfortable views on theatre. They became hugely popular for the same reasons.

Henrik Ibsen influenced the development of dramatic writing and performances to a degree that had not been seen since the theatre of William Shakespeare. Volumes have been written by academics and theatre scholars, interpreting his work in terms of psychological theses, Freudian concepts, mysticism, realism; from the viewpoints of more philosophies and theories possible to imagine. Dramaturgs and other theatre practitioners have researched and analysed each play down to the last comma, examining their theatricality and dramatic tension, their plots and stories and characterisations. Why is it that these middle-class drawing-room dramas still inspire directors to stage them and actors to play their characters?

Like all great literature, Ibsen's plays make something familiar 'new'. His drama throws a fresh perspective on a well-known story or situation or conflict. All great theatre draws us into the characters' world, whether it's a royal medieval court, a nineteenth-century Russian living-room or a garden on a Norwegian fjord.

In this introduction, the emphasis is on *Ellida* as a piece of theatre. For a very long time English-speaking people mostly read the plays or watched productions performed in British or American translations, often written in the light of psychological realism or the rise of naturalism in the late nineteenth century—theatre that attempts to create an illusion of reality. The most well-known, and well-regarded English versions, still read and produced today, are serious, often humourless, and frequently give rise to grave, earnest, sombre productions.[2] They tend to ignore any touch of comedy, Ibsen's wicked sense of irony, and the fact that he wrote at a time that was quickly moving towards expressionism in many art forms. His work inspired artists such as the Norwegian Edvard Munch, whose *Scream*—a painting of a world screaming in horror, pain and fear—expresses a mood or emotion underlying many of Ibsen's works. Yet his plays are also highly satirical, their irony revealing a world of quite another kind of life beneath the surface. An early play like *Peer Gynt* (1867) is as raucous, sexy and adventurous as Indiana Jones, except in verse; yet hauntingly despondent in its depiction of a man searching for something he has left at home without realising that's where his life is. *A Doll's House* and *Hedda Gabler* are both as satirical about the characters' deceitful society as Working Dog's TV series *Utopia*; and in their different ways, as heart-breaking as any Shakespearean tragedy. In the first play, Nora walks out on her husband and children; in the second, Hedda shoots herself in pure despair after her lover dies in a brothel. Yet both plays are full of funny, satirical moments. Similarly *Ghosts* is as comical in its depiction of the maid Regine, who tries to learn French so the young artist son of the house will take her with him to an exciting life in Paris, as it is tragic in its portrayal of a dying son asking his mother to help him out of his misery.

Where does *Ellida* fit into the Ibsen canon? I would claim that this play is as Ibsenite as anything he wrote. It has exciting characters offering challenges to actors, an intriguing story for directors to unravel, and the three productions I have seen prove that the play certainly inspires the imagination of all artists involved, including set and costume designers.

Once more the bourgeois family forms the core of the argument. Like Ellida (Mrs Wangel), most of Ibsen's women attempt to escape from their real selves, sometimes into a world of their own making, sometimes into a world fashioned for them by their husbands or by circumstances formed by their society. They are trapped in this world, living the kind of life their particular environment expects of them. The plays often deal with how these female characters go on a journey that opens up for new possibilities, making them realise that they are living a life created *for* them by well-meaning husbands rather than a life they have created themselves, for themselves. 'It is difficult to lie when you don't know the truth' a Norwegian director said in a seminar about his production of *The Lady from the Sea*. Doctor Wangel is truthful in his belief that he has given Ellida everything she needs, and that he has to protect her from the freedom she is longing for, the freedom to make her own choices. The journey towards truth is his as much as it is Ellida's.

The character of The Stranger has an aura of mystery. To Ellida he represents freedom because, as a seaman, he can leave the shore behind and journey across oceans. And what more of a romantic gesture than 'marrying' each other by throwing linked rings into the sea! But when Ellida breaks off their relationship, he refuses to accept it and continues to sail the seven seas. Ellida cannot quite get rid of him; to her, he still represents that unobtainable freedom that a life inside the fjords cannot offer. However, regardless of what he symbolises for Ellida, Ibsen doesn't even grant him the dignity of a name. He was a sailor when he left her and tourist when he returned – nothing more extraordinary than any other sailor or tourist.

The play opens on a bright late-summer morning. Bolette appears with a large vase of flowers; Ballested is busy hoisting the flag, his painting gear next to him; a young enthusiastic sculptor, Lyngstrand, turns up outside the fence; we hear that an old family friend, Arnholm, has arrived; the wife and mother of the house is on her way up from her early morning swim. But this pleasant atmosphere, a mixture of happy family events and artistic pursuits, is subtly undermined. The flowers are to celebrate the birthday of a dead mother and wife; Ballested has problems pronouncing the word 'acclimatise', suggesting he doesn't belong; Ellida's daily swim is a ritual which borders on the obsessive;

Lyngstrand has weak lungs and hopes to see the doctor. We also learn that the works of the two artists are far from inspired by the natural beauty surrounding them. Ballested's painting is of brackish fjord water with perishing mermaids, and Lyngstrand's group sculpture is of an unfaithful sea-wife whose drowned husband returns as a ghost-like figure.

All Ibsen's plays end in a question mark of some sort or another. In a sense, they are like thrillers moving mercilessly towards the solution of a conflict, which they fail to fully solve. In *A Doll's House*, what will happen to Nora after she has slammed the door behind her? When asked by his shocked contemporaries if she will return to her family, Ibsen answered 'How do I know?' Does Hedda's death change the insular thinking of the Tesman household? Will *Ghost's* Mrs Alving help her son to die?

So what are the questions at the end of *Ellida*? These are some of my own thoughts: Will Ellida and Wangel have a happy marriage after he has given her the freedom of choice? Most scholars seem critical of it. Yet she has freely accepted it. Like Ellida, Bolette accepts Arnholm's proposal of a life she could only dream of before, fully knowing what it involves. But are the 'freedoms' of Ellida and Bolette dearly bought? Are the dark and disturbing nature of Ballested's and Lyngstrand's art an ironic comment on their respective talents, or something more sinister about the reality around them? Is there in the final instance a sense of tragedy pointing towards an existence in which happiness and despair will always co-exist in an eternal struggle? There is certainly something ambiguous in Ballested's final line: 'The mermaid dies. Humans, on the other hand, can acc-acclimatise themselves.' However, for the first time, he gets the word 'acclimatise' right, apart from a slight stammer, suggesting that he, at last, may finally belong. But his stutter is still there. Maybe that is simply a comment on his art? Ultimately, perhaps the question in *Ellida* is really simple: will Ellida learn how to acclimatise herself? Despite its ambiguous nature, the ending suggests that she is willing to try, at least.

As the play concludes, the light Nordic summer is on the wane, the last tourist ship, carrying the Stranger, and the tourists with their money, disappears slowing and silently towards the open ocean. Soon 'all seaward passage shall be closed'. However, as the tourists disappear, the sound of the local brass band grow louder as it approaches the locals on the shore, the real life blood of the town. The tourists may leave, but the residents remain.

Finally, why did we change the title from *The Lady from the Sea* to the name of the main character? The original title is *Fruen fra havet*; 'frue' means wife in Norwegian, so literally, *The Wife from the Sea*. However, the Norwegian word for 'mermaid' is 'havfrue', so the title has a context impossible to achieve in English. 'Lady' may have worked in the late nineteenth century, when the first translation appeared, but not today. As Ellida is the wife from the sea, we chose to call the play after her character. Furthermore, 'Ellida' is her identity; the 'self' she is seeking to understand in the play, with its many possibilities, rather than the limiting label that the characters as well as the townspeople have bestowed on her.

After living in Germany and Italy for many years, Ibsen wanted to settle down at Öresund, on the coast between Denmark and Sweden: 'a free open space where I can see all the ocean-sailing ships come in from far away and sail out to far away places ... where do I find my homeland? The sea is what draws me the most.'[3] It was there that he wrote *Fruen fra havet*, *Ellida*.

## Endnotes

1       Henrik Ibsen, HU, volume 19, p. 172.
2       It should be noted that contemporary productions of classic plays are often adaptations written by a playwright or a director of a specific production.
4       Letter to Georg Brandes 3 June 1897. *Ibsen on Theatre*.

## Bibliography

*HU: Hundreårsutgaven* (*The Centenary Edition*), a collection of Henrik Ibsen's work in 22 volumes, edited by Francis Bull, Halvdan Koht and Didrik Arup Seip, 1928-1957, University of Oslo.
*Ibsen on Theatre*, edited by Julie Holledge and Frode Helland, translated by May-Brit Akerholt, to be published by Nick Hern Books, London, 2018.

# Postscript

Three new productions of plays by Ibsen open somewhere in the world every week. The frequency of global productions has steadily increased over the past thirty years. While Ibsen's plays have been associated historically with theatres of modernity, today they are adapted into multiple genres: Chinese and Western Opera forms, tourist spectacles, puppet plays, musicals, dance performances, Japanese Noh theatre, promenade performances, applied theatre, community events, and every possible screen technology. In addition to the plethora of global adaptations of his plays recorded in IbsenStage (performed in 8592 venues by 80,178 artists in 244 countries, and translated into 67 languages), Ibsen's dramas are included in educational curricula on five continents. (*IbsenStage Records* as of 1 March 2018).

*Ellida* was first produced by La Mama at the Courthouse Theatre, Melbourne, on 16 May 2018, with the following cast:

| | |
|---|---|
| BALLESTED | Dave Evans |
| BOLETTE | Meg Spencer |
| LYNGSTRAND | Martin Quinn |
| HILDE | Esther Myles |
| DR WANGEL | Jason Cavanagh |
| ARNHOLM | Gabriel Partington |
| ELLIDA | Annie Thorold |
| THE STRANGER | Frank Handrum |

Director, Laurence Strangio
Designer, Mattea Davies
Lighting designer, Georgia Stefania Rann
Musician, Dave Evans
Dramaturgy, May-Brit Akerholt, Laurence Strangio and Annie Thorold
Assistant director, Eva Justine Torkkola

## CHARACTERS

DR WANGEL

ELLIDA, his second wife

BOLETTE, his daughter by his first wife

HILDE, his younger daughter by his first wife

ARNHOLM, their former tutor

LYNGSTRAND, an aspiring artist

BALLESTED, bandmaster, barber, tour guide, painter, handyman

A STRANGER

## SETTING

The action takes place one Summer in a small town by a fjord in northern Norway.

This play went to press before the end of rehearsals and may differ from the play as performed.

# ACT ONE

*Dr Wangel's house, left, with a large roofed verandah. The house is surrounded by a garden. Below the verandah, a flagpole. In the garden, right, stands an arbour with table and chairs. Behind is a hedge with a little gate, and beyond is a roadway lined with trees. Through the trees can be seen the fjord and the peaks of high mountains in the distance. It is a hot, brilliantly clear summer morning.*

BALLESTED, *middle-aged, wearing an old velvet jacket and broad-brimmed artist's hat, is by the flagpole busy with the ropes. The flag is on the ground. Nearby is an easel with canvas on it. Beside it is a canvas chair on which lie brushes, a palette and a box of paints.*

BOLETTE WANGEL *comes out on the verandah through the open door. She is carrying a large vase of flowers which she puts on the table.*

BOLETTE: Well, Ballested? Can you manage to hoist it?

BALLESTED: Oh yes, Miss Wangel. Easy enough. May I ask, are you expecting visitors today?

BOLETTE: Yes.

BALLESTED: Strangers?

BOLETTE: Mr Arnholm. He arrived in town last night.

BALLESTED: Arnholm? That tutor we had here a few years ago?

BOLETTE: That's him.

BALLESTED: So he's come back here again. Well, well.

BOLETTE: That's why we're hoisting the flag.

BALLESTED: I suppose that's as good an occasion as any.

> BOLETTE *returns to the garden room. A few moments later,* LYNGSTRAND *comes walking along the road from the right, stops, interested, when he sees the easel and artist's materials. He is a thin young man, poorly but neatly dressed, and of delicate appearance.*

LYNGSTRAND: [*from outside the hedge*] Good morning.

BALLESTED: Oh! Good morning. [*Hoists the flag*] There! Up up and away! [*Moving over to the easel*] I don't think I've had the pleasure—?

LYNGSTRAND: So you're a painter.

BALLESTED: And why shouldn't I be a painter?

LYNGSTRAND: Why shouldn't you. Could I come in for a look?

BALLESTED: There's not a lot to see yet. But please.

LYNGSTRAND *enters through the gate.*

BALLESTED: [*painting*] I'm working on the fjord between the small islands.

LYNGSTRAND: So I see.

BALLESTED: But the figure's still missing. Can't find a single model.

LYNGSTRAND: So there'll be a figure as well?

BALLESTED: Lying among the rocks in the foreground there'll be a dying mermaid.

LYNGSTRAND: Why is she dying?

BALLESTED: She has strayed in from the open sea and can't find her way back. So she's lying there, perishing in the brackish fjord water.

LYNGSTRAND: Oh, I see.

BALLESTED: It was the doctor's wife who gave me the idea.

LYNGSTRAND: What are you going to call it when it's finished?

BALLESTED: I intend to call it 'The Passing of the Mermaid'.

LYNGSTRAND: Seems appropriate. I'm sure that'll make a fine picture.

BALLESTED: [*looking at him*] A colleague, perhaps?

LYNGSTRAND: Not exactly. I'm going to be a sculptor. My name's Hans Lyngstrand.

BALLESTED: A sculptor, so that's your choice? Been here long?

LYNGSTRAND: About a fortnight. But I hope to stay for the rest of the summer.

BALLESTED: To enjoy the sea and the sun, eh?

LYNGSTRAND: I need to build up my strength.

BALLESTED: Of delicate health, are you?

LYNGSTRAND: Nothing to worry about. Just a bit short of breath. My chest.

BALLESTED: Mere bagatelle! Still, you should have a chat with our doctor.

LYNGSTRAND: Yes, I was hoping to consult Dr Wangel.

BALLESTED: Good idea. [*Looks left*] There's another steamer. There's been such an increase of summer visitors over the last few years. I fear our little town is going to lose its character with all these strangers arriving.

LYNGSTRAND: You were born here?

BALLESTED: Oh no. But I've accalo— acclimatised myself.

LYNGSTRAND: You've lived here a long time then?

BALLESTED: Eighteen years or so. I arrived with Skive's touring theatre. I was doing decoration and design. But the company broke up and we scattered to the four winds.

LYNGSTRAND: But you remained?

BALLESTED: I remained.

> BOLETTE *comes out with a rocking chair which she puts on the verandah.*

BOLETTE: [*calling*] Hilde! See if you can find the embroidered footstool for father.

LYNGSTRAND: [*walking up to the verandah*] Good morning, Miss Wangel!

BOLETTE: Oh, Mr Lyngstrand! Good morning. Excuse me, I'll just—

> *She goes into the house.*

BALLESTED: You know the family then?

LYNGSTRAND: Not really. I've met the daughter on the odd occasion. And I spoke with the doctor's wife at the concert up on the lookout. She said I was welcome to come and visit. All I need is the right occasion.

BALLESTED: [*looking out, left*] Damn it! The steamer's at the quay already.

> *He starts to collect his things.*

I must get down to the hotel. Some of the arrivals may want my services. I'm a hairdresser too, you know.

LYNGSTRAND: A man of many talents.

BALLESTED: You have to acli— acclimatise yourself in a small place like this. Should you need anything in the way of hair … some shampoo perhaps … just ask for Dance Master Ballested.

LYNGSTRAND: Dance Master?

BALLESTED: And President of the Brass Band Society. We've got a concert at the lookout tonight. Goodbye! Goodbye!

> *He walks out the garden gate, to the left.* HILDE *comes out with the footstool.* BOLETTE *brings more flowers.* LYNGSTRAND *greets* HILDE *from the garden. At the railing,* HILDE *doesn't acknowledge his greeting.*

HILDE: Bolette said you'd actually ventured inside the gate.

LYNGSTRAND: Yes, I took the liberty.

HILDE: Been out for a morning walk, have you?

LYNGSTRAND: Not really. Not much of a walk anyway.

HILDE: Had a swim, perhaps?

LYNGSTRAND: Yes, I went for a little swim in the sea. I saw your mother down there. She went into her bathing hut.

HILDE: Who?

LYNGSTRAND: Your mother.

HILDE: I see.

> *She puts the footstool in front of the rocking chair.*

BOLETTE: [*cutting in*] Did you happen to see Father's boat out on the fjord?

LYNGSTRAND: I thought I saw his sailboat heading back in.

HILDE: He's been visiting patients on the islands.

> *She arranges things on the table.*

LYNGSTRAND: [*putting a foot on the steps*] What a festival of flowers!

BOLETTE: Doesn't it look nice?

LYNGSTRAND: Are you celebrating something?

HILDE: We certainly are.

LYNGSTRAND: Your father's birthday, is it?

BOLETTE: [*to* HILDE, *warningly*] Hm. Hm.

HILDE: [*ignoring her*] No, Mother's.

LYNGSTRAND: Oh I see! Your mother's.

BOLETTE: [*low, angry voice*] Hilde!

HILDE: [*in a similar voice*] Leave me alone! [*To* LYNGSTRAND] I expect you'll go home and have your breakfast now?

LYNGSTRAND *takes a step down.*

LYNGSTRAND: I suppose I should get some food into me?

HILDE: I'm sure you live pretty well down at the hotel?

LYNGSTRAND: I don't live at the hotel anymore. It got too expensive.

HILDE: Where do you live now?

LYNGSTRAND: Up at Mrs Jensen's.

HILDE *looks questioningly at him.*

The midwife.

HILDE: Excuse me, but I do have other things to see to …

LYNGSTRAND: Perhaps I shouldn't have said that. What I said.

HILDE *looks him up and down with disdain.* BOLETTE *comes down the steps.*

BOLETTE: I'm sorry Mr Lyngstrand. You have to excuse us for now. Another day—when you have time, and when you feel like it—please do drop in and say hello to Father and—and the rest of us.

LYNGSTRAND: Thank you. I'd like that very much.

LYNGSTRAND *raises his hat and walks out through the garden gate. As he walks along the path, left, he raises his hat again towards the verandah.*

HILDE: [*half aloud*] Adieu, monsieur! And give my best wishes to old mother Jensen.

BOLETTE: [*quietly, shaking her arm*] Hilde! Have you gone mad? What if he heard you?

HILDE: So what! Do you think I care?

BOLETTE *looks out right.*

BOLETTE: Here's Father.

DR WANGEL, *in travelling clothes, carrying a small bag, comes up the path, right.*

WANGEL: Here I am, girls, all yours again!

*He walks through the garden gate.* BOLETTE *goes down to meet him.*

BOLETTE: It's lovely to have you back!

HILDE: Have you finished for the day then?

WANGEL: I'm afraid I have to go down to the surgery later. Just briefly. Do you know if Arnholm has arrived?

BOLETTE: He arrived last night. We asked at the hotel.

HILDE: [*pulling his arm*] Father, look, look!

WANGEL: [*looking at the verandah*] Yes I see, dear. It's very festive.

BOLETTE: Haven't we made it look nice!

WANGEL: Yes. Are we ... are we alone in the house now?

HILDE: Yes, she's gone—

BOLETTE: [*quickly*] Mother's gone for a swim.

> WANGEL *looks affectionately at* BOLETTE, *pats her head. Awkwardly.*

WANGEL: Listen, my girls, do you want to leave it like this for the whole day? With the flag flying as well?

HILDE: Of course we do, Father!

WANGEL: Well. Yes. Alright. But ...

> BOLETTE *blinks and nods.*

BOLETTE: Surely you know we've done it all for Mr Arnholm? When such a good friend visits us for the first time in—

> HILDE *smiles and shakes his arm.*

HILDE: After all, he was Bolette's tutor!

WANGEL: [*half-smiling*] You're a cunning pair aren't you ... Oh well. We still must remember her, although she's no longer with us. Here, Hilde. [*He gives her the bag*] Could you put this in my surgery? But you see ... I don't like this. Every year. Afraid I don't. However. If you must.

> HILDE *is about to leave with the bag through the garden, left, but stops and points.*

HILDE: Look, that man over there. Isn't that the headmaster?

BOLETTE: [*looking*] What, him? [*He laughs.*] Don't be silly! That middle-aged man!

WANGEL: Arnholm? Yes so it is!

BOLETTE: [*staring, amazed*] Good God, I think you're right!

ARNHOLM, *elegantly dressed in morning clothes, gold spectacles and with a slender cane, comes up the path from the left. He looks tired, strained. He looks into the garden, gives them a friendly wave and comes through the gate.* WANGEL *goes to meet him.*

WANGEL: Welcome, my dear Arnholm. Welcome back to to your old neighbourhood.

ARNHOLM: Thank you, Dr Wangel. Very kind of you.

*The two men shake hands warmly and come back across the garden together.*

I'd hardly have recognised you two.

WANGEL: I'd be surprised if you did.

ARNHOLM: Except—Bolette, perhaps. Yes, I think I'd recognise you, Bolette.

WANGEL: Really? It's been eight or nine years since you last saw her. I dare say much has changed since then.

ARNHOLM: [*looking around*] Not really. Except the trees have grown taller, and you've built that arbour—

WANGEL: That's just the look of things—

ARNHOLM: [*smiling*] And now you have two eligible, grown-up daughters!

WANGEL: One, at least.

HILDE: [*half loud voice*] Father, really!

WANGEL: Why don't we sit up on the verandah? It's nice and cool there.

*He gestures to the verandah.*

ARNHOLM: Thank you, Dr Wangel.

*They go up.* WANGEL *indicates the rocking chair to* ARNHOLM.

BOLETTE: [*to* WANGEL] Should we serve some juice and soda water in the garden room? It'll soon be too hot out here.

WANGEL: Why not? And perhaps a little cognac?

BOLETTE: Cognac as well?

WANGEL: Just a small glass. If someone should want some …

BOLETTE: Yes. Hilde, take Father's bag down to the surgery.

BOLETTE *goes into the garden room, closes the door.* ARNHOLM *watches her leave.* HILDE *takes the bag out through the garden and behind the house, left.*

ARNHOLM: What a splendid—two splendid girls they've become.

WANGEL: [*sitting*] Yes, I think so.

ARNHOLM: I'm especially surprised over Bolette—and Hilde too, of course. But what about you Doctor? You plan to live here the rest of your life?

WANGEL: I suppose. Here's where I'm born and bred, as they say. I was so happy here, so incredibly happy with her—with my wife—but she left us too early.

ARNHOLM: Yes. I remember her.

WANGEL: And now I live here so happily with the one who took her place. Life has treated me well … on the whole.

ARNHOLM: No children in your second marriage?

WANGEL: We had a little boy, almost three years ago now. But he died, just five months old.

*Pause.*

ARNHOLM: Isn't your wife at home today?

WANGEL: She should be here soon. She has gone down to the fjord for a swim. She does that every day at this time of year, whatever the weather.

ARNHOLM: Oh? Is something wrong?

WANGEL: I can't quite place what's wrong. She has had some problems with her nerves these last few years. But it seems that swimming in the sea makes her feel happier.

ARNHOLM: Yes, I do remember.

WANGEL: [*with a slight smile*] Of course, you used to know Ellida when you were teaching out there in Skjoldviken.

ARNHOLM: Yes. She would often call in at the vicarage. But I mostly met her out at her father's—at the lighthouse.

WANGEL: Those years out there have set their mark on her. People here don't understand her. They call her 'the woman from the sea'.

ARNHOLM: Do they really?

WANGEL: Yes. Perhaps you could talk to her about those days, Arnholm? It would do her a world of good.

ARNHOLM: [*looking doubtfully at him*] Do you think so?

WANGEL: I do.

ELLIDA: [*offstage, from the garden, right*] Wangel? Are you there?

WANGEL: [*standing up*] Yes, my dear.

> MRS ELLIDA WANGEL *enters through the trees by the arbour. She is wearing a large, light wrap and her wet hair hangs loose over her shoulders.* ARNHOLM *stands up.*

[*Smiling, he holds his hands out to her*] The return of the mermaid!

ELLIDA: [*walking quickly up to the verandah and grabbing his hands*] Thank God. I'm so glad to see you. When did you get back?

WANGEL: A few minutes ago. [*Indicates* ARNHOLM] Don't you want to say hello to an old friend?

ELLIDA: You're here! Welcome! Forgive me for not being at home …

ARNHOLM: Oh please! Don't go to any trouble for me.

WANGEL: How was the water today? Nice and fresh?

ELLIDA: Fresh! God no, the water's never fresh here. Luke warm and lethargic. The water here in the fjords is sick.

ARNHOLM: Sick?

ELLIDA: Yes, sick. And it infects us too, makes us sick.

WANGEL: [*smiling*] There's a fine recommendation for our holiday resort.

ARNHOLM: Still, I believe that you, Mrs Wangel, have a special affinity with the open sea, and everything to do with it.

ELLIDA: Maybe. Sometimes I think I do… Oh, look at the display the girls have arranged for you.

WANGEL: Hm. I think I'd better—

ARNHOLM: Is it really for me?

ELLIDA: Yes of course. Surely you don't think we decorate like this every day? Oh, it's so stifling under this roof. [*She goes down into the garden.*] Come! At least there's a suggestion of a breeze over here.

> *She sits down in the arbour.*

ARNHOLM: [*walking across*] To me the air seems very fresh.

ELLIDA: You're used to the stuffy air in the capital. I've heard it's suffocating in summer.

WANGEL *joins her in the garden.*

WANGEL: Ellida, my dear, I'm afraid you'll have to entertain our friend by yourself for a while.

ELLIDA: You have work to do?

WANGEL: Yes, I have to take a quick trip to the surgery. And then I have to get changed. But I won't be long.

ARNHOLM *sits down in the arbour.*

ARNHOLM: Please don't hurry, your wife and I will find ways to pass the time.

WANGEL *nods.*

WANGEL: Yes. I trust you will. I'll see you later.

WANGEL *goes out through the garden, left.*

ELLIDA: [*after a short pause*] It's pleasant, sitting out here, don't you think?

ARNHOLM: Yes, very pleasant.

ELLIDA: They call this *my* arbour. Because I created it. Or rather, Wangel made it, for me.

ARNHOLM: And you like to sit out here?

ELLIDA: Yes, I spend most days here.

ARNHOLM: With the girls?

ELLIDA: No. The girls … they prefer the verandah.

ARNHOLM: And Wangel?

ELLIDA: Oh Wangel comes and goes between us. Sometimes here with me, sometimes over there with the children.

ARNHOLM: Is that how you want it?

ELLIDA: I think we are all more comfortable like that. We can call across to each other—if we have something to say.

ARNHOLM: [*after a moment's thought*] The last time our paths crossed— out in Skjoldviken. Well. It's a long time ago now …

ELLIDA: It must be ten years since you were out there.

ARNHOLM: Something like that. But when I think about you, out there in the lighthouse! The 'heathen', as the old priest called you, because he thought your father had given you the name of a ship instead of a proper Christian name.

ELLIDA: Yes. So?

ARNHOLM: I would never have thought I'd find you here as Mrs Wangel.

ELLIDA: Wangel wasn't—the girls' mother was still alive then. Their real mother.

ARNHOLM: Yes, of course. Yes. But even if he had been—free, I could never have imagined the two of you …

ELLIDA: Nor could I. Not then.

ARNHOLM: The doctor is a good man. Respectable. Genuinely kind to everyone—

ELLIDA: [*warmly and sincerely*] Yes, he certainly is.

ARNHOLM: But surely, you two must be worlds apart.

ELLIDA: That's true. We are.

ARNHOLM: So how did it happen? How come you—

ELLIDA: Please Arnholm, you mustn't ask me. I couldn't even begin to explain. And even if I could, you'd never be able to understand.

ARNHOLM: Hm. Did you ever confide in your husband about me? You know. My clumsy attempt—

ELLIDA: Of course not! I haven't mentioned a word about that.

ARNHOLM: I'm glad to hear it. Because I felt a bit, you know, awkward at the thought that—

ELLIDA: There's absolutely no need. I've only told him the truth, that I was very fond of you and that you were the best friend I had out there.

ARNHOLM: I appreciate that. But why did you never write to me after I left?

ELLIDA: I thought perhaps it might hurt you to hear from someone who—who couldn't return your feelings. I thought it might be like ripping open old wounds.

ARNHOLM: Yes. You may well be right.

ELLIDA: But why didn't you write?

ARNHOLM: [*looking at her, smiling reproachfully*] Me? Take the first step? Raise the suspicion that I wanted to try again? After the rejection you had given me?

ELLIDA: No, of course. But have you never thought of finding someone else?

ARNHOLM: I've remained faithful to my memories.

ELLIDA: [*half in jest*] Oh come on! Let go of those sad old memories. Better to think about making some woman a good husband.

ARNHOLM: At my age? I've just turned thirty-seven, you know.

ELLIDA: All the more reason to hurry. [*She is silent for a moment, then, earnestly, in a low voice*] Listen. I can tell you something now that I couldn't say then, even if my life depended on it.

ARNHOLM: What's that?

ELLIDA: When you made what you call your clumsy attempt—there was no way I could have answered you differently.

ARNHOLM: I know. All you had to offer me was friendship.

ELLIDA: What you don't know is that my heart, all my thoughts, were with someone else.

ARNHOLM: How can that be possible? You didn't know Wangel then, did you?

ELLIDA: I'm not talking about Wangel.

ARNHOLM: If not Wangel … there was no-one out there you could possibly have been interested in.

ELLIDA: Yes. No. Everything was so confusing. All you need to know is that I wasn't free.

ARNHOLM: And if you had been? Would you've answered me differently?

ELLIDA: How can I know? When Wangel appeared, the answer was different.

ARNHOLM: Why tell me about this now?

ELLIDA *rises nervously, seemingly distressed.*

ELLIDA: Because I need someone to confide in. No, don't get up.

ARNHOLM: So your husband knows nothing about this other man?

ELLIDA: I confessed to him that my feelings had once belonged to someone else. He has never asked for more. And we've never touched on it since. Madness, that's all it was. And it all soon fell apart. In a way, at least.

ARNHOLM: [*rises*] In a way?

ELLIDA: Altogether! Oh Arnholm, it's not at all what you think. I don't know how to begin to tell you. You'd think I was sick. Or gone totally mad.

ARNHOLM: You must tell me everything. I insist.

ELLIDA: I'll try. How would you, a sensible man, understand that— [*Looking out, she interrupts herself*] Let's wait. Someone's coming.

LYNGSTRAND *is coming on the road, left, walking into the garden. He has a flower in his buttonhole and carries a large, impressive bouquet, wrapped in paper and tied with ribbons. He stops and hesitates at the verandah.*

[*From the arbour*] Are you looking for the girls, Mr Lyngstrand?

*He turns to her.*

LYNGSTRAND: Oh, good morning, there you are. [*He goes over to join them.*] No, it's you I want, Mrs Wangel. You did say I could could come for a visit—?

ELLIDA: Of course. You're always welcome here.

LYNGSTRAND: Thank you. And as it turns out to be a special day of celebration—

ELLIDA: So you know, do you?

LYNGSTRAND: I certainly do. So I take the liberty of presenting you with—

*He bows and hands her the bouquet of flowers.*

ELLIDA: [*smiling*] But dear Mr Lyngstrand, shouldn't you give your beautiful flowers to our visitor, Mr Arnholm?

LYNGSTRAND: [*looking uncertainly at them both*] Forgive me, but … this gentleman's a stranger to me. I'm here in connection with the birthday.

ELLIDA: The birthday? I'm afraid there's been a mistake, there's no birthday here today.

LYNGSTRAND: [*smiling knowingly*] I didn't know it was supposed to be a secret.

ELLIDA: What's a secret?

LYNGSTRAND: That today's your birthday, Mrs Wangel.

ELLIDA: Mine? Where did you get that from?

LYNGSTRAND: Hilde let it slip when I dropped in earlier and asked why all the flowers and flags and—

ELLIDA: And?

LYNGSTRAND: And Hilde said, today's Mother's birthday.

ELLIDA: Mother's! Ah.

ARNHOLM: Aha!

> *He and* ELLIDA *exchange a glance of understanding.*

Well, now that this young man has found out ...

ELLIDA: [*to* LYNGSTRAND] Yes, now that you managed to find out ...

LYNGSTRAND: [*offering her the bouquet again*] Please accept my congratulations.

> ELLIDA *takes the flowers.*

ELLIDA: Thank you so much. Please, won't you sit down for a moment?

> ELLIDA, ARNHOLM *and* LYNGSTRAND *sit down in the arbour.*

All this about—my birthday—it was meant to be a secret, Mr Arnholm.

ARNHOLM: Not for us outsiders.

> ELLIDA *puts the flowers on the table.*

ELLIDA: That's right. Not for outsiders.

LYNGSTRAND: I won't mention it to a living soul.

ELLIDA: No matter. [*Pause*] You're looking better these days, Mr Lyngstrand.

LYNGSTRAND: Yes, I think I'm improving. And by next year, if I can travel south to a warmer climate, maybe ...

ELLIDA: And you will, the girls were telling me.

LYNGSTRAND: Yes, because I have a benefactor in Bergen who looks after me. And he's promised to help me next year.

ELLIDA: How did you find him?

LYNGSTRAND: I was so lucky. I was at sea in one of his ships at one stage.

ELLIDA: Really? You wanted to go to sea?

LYNGSTRAND: Not at all. But after my mother died, my father didn't want me hanging around. So he sent me off to sea. We were shipwrecked in the English Channel on the way home. And that was lucky for me!

ARNHOLM: That was lucky?

LYNGSTRAND: Yes. That's when my health was damaged. My chest. I was in the freezing water for a very long time before they rescued me. I had to give up the sea. Which turned out to be my good luck. The damage wasn't really dangerous. And so now I can become a sculptor, something I've always wanted. Imagine, moulding that lovely clay, feeling it forming beneath your fingers!

ELLIDA: And what would you like to form? Seamen and mermaids? Or old Vikings, perhaps?

LYNGSTRAND: No, nothing like that. As soon as my health allows, I'll try to create a big piece. A group composition, as they call it.

ELLIDA: I see. And what will the group represent?

LYNGSTRAND: Something from my own experience.

ELLIDA: What will it be?

LYNGSTRAND: What I have in mind is the sleeping figure of a young sea-wife, strangely restless, yet dreaming. I should be able to make it look as if she is dreaming.

ARNHOLM: Shouldn't there be more to it?

LYNGSTRAND: Yes, another figure. A 'gestalt', they call it.

ARNHOLM: A ghostly shape?

LYNGSTRAND: That'll be her husband, who she's been unfaithful to while he was away. And he has drowned at sea.

ARNHOLM: Drowned?

ELLIDA: Did he drown?

LYNGSTRAND: Yes. He drowned on a sea voyage. But the strange thing is that he has returned home even so. It is late at night. And now he stands at the bedside, looking at her. He'll stand there dripping wet like a drowned man dredged up from the sea depths.

ELLIDA: [*leaning back in her chair*] What a strange vision. [*She closes her eyes*] You've brought it alive for me.

ARNHOLM: But how on earth, Mr—Mr—! You said it should be something you yourself have experienced.

LYNGSTRAND: I don't mean directly experienced. Not personally as such. But still …

ELLIDA: [*lively, tense*] Tell me everything!

LYNGSTRAND: When our ship was to sail from a town called Halifax, we had to leave the bosun at the hospital there. In his place we signed on an American. This new bosun—

ELLIDA: The American?

LYNGSTRAND: Yes. He kept browsing newspapers he borrowed from the captain. He told us he wanted to learn Norwegian.

ELLIDA: What happened then?

LYNGSTRAND: Then, one dark night, there was a violent storm, and all the men were up on deck. All except the new bosun and me. He'd sprained his foot, and I was lying on my bunk, feeling awful. Well, he sat there in the cabin reading one of the old newspapers—

ELLIDA: Yes, yes?

LYNGSTRAND: And I hear him uttering a sort of howl. And I see that his face is as white as chalk. He starts to crush and crumble the paper, tearing it to a thousand shreds. But he did it so quietly, so very quietly.

ELLIDA: He didn't say anything?

LYNGSTRAND: Not at first. But after a while he said to himself: 'Married. To another. While I was away.'

ELLIDA *shuts her eyes.*

ELLIDA: [*in a low voice*] He said that?

LYNGSTRAND: He did. And imagine, he said it in really good Norwegian! He must have a flair for languages, that man.

ELLIDA: What then? What else happened?

LYNGSTRAND: Ah! Then came the strangest part. He continued in the same quiet voice: 'But she is mine, and she will always be mine. And she will follow me, if I have to come back for her like a man drowned in the depths of the black black sea.'

ELLIDA *pours herself a glass of water, her hand trembling. She exhales.*

ELLIDA: How stifling the air is today …

LYNGSTRAND: And he said it with such a determined force that I thought he would be man enough to do it.

ELLIDA: Do you know anything more? About what has become of that man?

LYNGSTRAND: Oh Mrs Wangel, I'd be surprised if he's still alive.

ELLIDA: [*quickly*] Why is that?

LYNGSTRAND: Because after that, we were shipwrecked in the Channel.

ELLIDA: And nothing has been heard of him since?

LYNGSTRAND: Neither sight nor sound, I believe. That's why I feel so strongly about turning it into a work of art. She's so alive to me, this unfaithful sea-wife—and the drowned avenger who still returns from the sea. I can see them both, so vividly.

ELLIDA: So can I. [*She stands up*] Come, let's go inside. Or better still, down to Wangel! I'm suffocating.

ELLIDA *leaves the arbour.* LYNGSTRAND *stands up as well.*

LYNGSTRAND: I'd better be off. I only came for a quick visit to offer my congratulations.

ELLIDA: [*offering him her hand*] Thank you for the flowers.

LYNGSTRAND *shakes her hand and goes out through the garden gate, left.* ARNHOLM *stands up and walks over to* ELLIDA.

ARNHOLM: I can see that this has touched you deeply.

ELLIDA: Yes. Although—

ARNHOLM: But surely you must have been prepared.

ELLIDA: Prepared? For someone to return … to return like that!

ARNHOLM: What on earth! Surely that deranged sculptor's sea yarn—?

ELLIDA: He may not be all that deranged.

ARNHOLM: So it's the tale of the dead man that's shaken you? I thought you were just pretending. Covering up the discovery of this secret family celebration. Knowing your husband and his children are living a life of memories without including you.

ELLIDA: No. No, I have no right to demand that my husband is mine and mine alone.

ARNHOLM: I think you do have that right.

ELLIDA: Yes. Yet I don't. That's how matters stand. I myself have something in my life from which the others are excluded.

ARNHOLM: You do? [*Lowering his voice*] Am I to understand—? You don't—don't love your husband!

ELLIDA: Yes I do. I've come to love him with all my heart! That's why it's so terrible—so inexplicable, so completely unthinkable!

ARNHOLM: You have to tell me what's making you so unhappy! Please?

ELLIDA: I can't. Not now. Later, perhaps.

> BOLETTE *comes out on the verandah and goes down into the garden.*

BOLETTE: Father's coming back from the surgery. Shouldn't we all sit down together in the garden room?

ELLIDA: Yes, let's.

> WANGEL, *having changed his clothes, enters with* HILDE *from behind the house, left.*

WANGEL: Here you have me again! I'm all yours! And more than ready for something in a nice cool glass.

ELLIDA: Just a moment.

> *She goes into the arbour and collects the flowers.*

HILDE: What lovely flowers! Where did you get them?

ELLIDA: I got them from Mr Lyngstrand, Hilde.

HILDE: [*starts*] Lyngstrand?

BOLETTE: [*uneasily*] Has Lyngstrand been here … again?

ELLIDA: [*half-smiling*] Yes. He brought these with him. In honour of the birthday, he said.

BOLETTE: [*glaring at* HILDE ] Oh!

HILDE: [*mumbling*] The idiot!

WANGEL: [*painfully embarrassed*] Well, you see ... My dearest Ellida, I just—

ELLIDA: [*interrupting*] Come, girls! Let's put the flowers in a vase with all the others.

> ELLIDA *walks up on the verandah.*

BOLETTE: [*to* HILDE *, low voice*] See. She's really quite nice after all.

HILDE: [*half-loud, angrily*] Monkey-tricks! She's just pretending, to charm father.

*On the verandah,* WANGEL *squeezes* ELLIDA*'s hand.*

WANGEL: Thank you, Ellida, thank you. I'm so very grateful.

ELLIDA: [*arranging the flowers*] Oh well, shouldn't I, too, be included in celebrating—Mother's birthday?

ARNHOLM: Hm.

*He goes to join* WANGEL *and* ELLIDA. BOLETTE *and* HILDE *remain down in the garden.*

# ACT TWO

*Up on the lookout, a wooded height behind the town. In the background there is a cairn and a weathervane. In the foreground and surrounding the cairn are large stones arranged as seats. Far below in the background we see the outer fjord, with islands and headlands. The open ocean cannot be seen. A summer evening, dusk. There is a reddish-gold glow in the air and on the distant mountain peaks. The sound of a four-part song can be heard faintly from the slopes below, right.*

*Young people from the town, men and women, come up in couples from the right; talking intimately, they walk past the cairn and out, left. A few seconds later,* BALLESTED *enters as guide to a party of foreign tourists and their ladies. He is weighed down with shawls and bags.*

BALLESTED: [*pointing upwards with his stick. In German*] *Sehen Sie, meine Herrshaften, dort liegt eine andere hill. Das willen wir also besteigen, et au-dessous de ...*

    BALLESTED *continues in French and leads the party out left.* HILDE *comes quickly up the slope, right, stops and looks back. A moment later,* BOLETTE *follows.*

BOLETTE: Hilde! Why do we keep running away from Lyngstrand?

HILDE: Because I hate walking so slowly uphill. Look how he's almost crawling upwards.

BOLETTE: You know how frail he is.

HILDE: Do you think it's really serious?

BOLETTE: Yes, I do.

HILDE: He was in Father's surgery this afternoon. I'd love to know what Father thinks.

BOLETTE: Father told me it's a hardening of the lung—or something like that. He's not long for this world, in his opinion.

HILDE: Imagine, that's exactly what I've been thinking.

BOLETTE: For God's sake, don't tell him.

HILDE: What do you take me for? [*Low voice*] Look, Hans has finally managed to scramble up. Hans—he looks like a Hans, don't you think?

BOLETTE: [*whispering*] Behave yourself. I'm warning you!

LYNGSTRAND *enters, right, carrying a parasol.*

LYNGSTRAND: Forgive me, please, I don't seem to walk as fast as you.

HILDE: You've got yourself a parasol, I see?

LYNGSTRAND: It's your mother's. She told me to use it as a walking stick. I didn't bring one.

BOLETTE: Are they still down there? Father and the others?

LYNGSTRAND: Yes. Your father ducked into the refreshment area. The others are sitting outside listening to the music. But your mother said they would come up later.

HILDE: [*looking at him*] You must be very tired by now.

LYNGSTRAND: Yes, I think I'd like to sit down for a moment.

*He sits on a stone in the foreground, right.*

HILDE: [*standing in front of him*] Do you know there's going to be dancing later, down at the bandstand?

LYNGSTRAND: I heard talk of it.

HILDE: Don't you think dancing is great fun?

BOLETTE: [*picking wildflowers among the heather*] Hilde! Let Mr Lyngstrand get his breath back.

LYNGSTRAND: [*to* HILDE ] Yes, I would love to dance. If only I could.

HILDE: Oh. Did you never learn?

LYNGSTRAND: No, I never learnt either. But I was talking about my chest.

HILDE: Because of this … frailty of yours?

LYNGSTRAND: Yes, because of that.

HILDE: Does your frail chest make you very sad?

LYNGSTRAND: I wouldn't say that. [*He smiles.*] Because that's why everyone's so kind and friendly and helpful to me.

HILDE: And of course, it's not the least bit dangerous either.

LYNGSTRAND: Not dangerous at all, as your father made clear to me.

HILDE: Besides, it'll go away once you travel to the south.

LYNGSTRAND: Yes. Then it'll go away.

BOLETTE: [*offering flowers*] Here, Mr Lyngstrand, these are for your buttonhole.

LYNGSTRAND: Thank you so much, Miss Bolette, how kind of you.

HILDE: [*looking down, right*] Here they come.

BOLETTE: [*looking down*] Oh no, they're taking the wrong turn!

LYNGSTRAND: I'll run down and shout to them.

HILDE: You'll have to shout very loudly.

BOLETTE: You'll only get tired again.

LYNGSTRAND: All downhill—smooth sailing.

> *He exits, right.*

BOLETTE: Poor man.

HILDE: If Lyngstrand proposed to you, would you accept?

BOLETTE: Are you out of your mind?

HILDE: I mean, if he didn't have this—frailty. And if he wasn't going to die soon. Would you have him then?

BOLETTE: I think it'd be better if you had him.

HILDE: Don't be silly. He doesn't have a peanut to his name. Not even enough to keep himself alive.

BOLETTE: So why are you always carrying on about him?

HILDE: Only because of his frailty.

BOLETTE: I haven't noticed you feeling sorry for him.

HILDE: I don't. But it's so tempting, somehow.

BOLETTE: Tempting?

HILDE: To watch him while he's telling me that it's not dangerous. That he'll be given a trip abroad, and that he's going to be an artist. He keeps believing it all, and he's so delighted about it. But nothing will come of it. He won't live long enough. I find that quite thrilling somehow.

BOLETTE: Thrilling?

HILDE: That's right. Thrilling. Now I've said it.

BOLETTE: You, Hilde Wangel, are a shameless, nasty girl.

HILDE: Yes. I want to be. Spiteful! [*Looking down the hill*] It doesn't look as if Arnholm's enjoying the climb. [*She turns around*] Do you know what I noticed about him at dinner? His hair's falling out. He's going bald!

BOLETTE: Rubbish.

HILDE: He is. And he's got wrinkles around both eyes. My God, Bolette, how could you've fallen for him when he was teaching you?

BOLETTE: [*smiling*] Yes, it's hard to understand. I remember bursting into tears once because he thought Bolette was an ugly name.

HILDE: Ha! [*Looking down*] Look at that! Now the 'woman from the sea' is talking with him. Not with Father. I wonder if there's something going on between those two.

BOLETTE: You should be ashamed of yourself. How can you say such a thing?

HILDE: Believe what you want. We'll never get along. She's not our kind, we're not her kind. God knows why father dragged her into the house! I wouldn't be surprised if she lost her mind completely one day.

BOLETTE: What on earth makes you think that?

HILDE: What's strange about that? Her mother went mad, too. She died a loony, I know that.

BOLETTE: God knows there isn't much you don't stick your nose into. But please keep your mouth shut, for Father's sake. Do you hear?

WANGEL, ELLIDA, ARNHOLM *and* LYNGSTRAND *enter, right.*

ELLIDA: [*pointing*] Out there it lies. Out there lies the open sea.

BOLETTE: [*to* ARNHOLM] Isn't it beautiful up here?

ARNHOLM: It's magnificent. Wonderful view.

WANGEL: You haven't been up here before, have you?

ARNHOLM: No. In my time I don't think there was even a path.

WANGEL: We've been taming the wilderness these last few years.

BOLETTE: Over there, at the crow's nest, the view's even more stunning.

WANGEL: Shall we walk over there, Ellida?

ELLIDA: [*sitting down on a rock, right*] Not me, thanks. But why don't the rest of you go.

WANGEL: I'll stay with you. The girls can show Mr Arnholm around.

BOLETTE: Do you fancy coming with us, Mr Arnholm?

ARNHOLM: Indeed I do. Have they made a path up there, too?

BOLETTE: Oh yes, a good wide path.

HILDE: So wide that two people can walk arm in arm.

ARNHOLM: [*jokingly*] Is that so, Miss Hilde! [*To* BOLETTE] Would you like to see if she's right?

BOLETTE: [*suppressing a smile*] Yes. Let's.

*They walk out, left, arm in arm.*

HILDE: [*to* LYNGSTRAND] Would you like a walk as well?

LYNGSTRAND: Arm in arm?

HILDE: Why not?

LYNGSTRAND: [*taking her arm, laughing happily*] This is a bit of a lark, isn't it!

HILDE: A lark?

LYNGSTRAND: Well, it looks as if we're engaged! Perhaps …

HILDE: Have you never walked arm in arm with a woman before?

*They go out, left.*

WANGEL: Well, Ellida, dear, finally we have a moment to ourselves.

ELLIDA: Yes. Come here and sit with me.

WANGEL: [*sitting*] It's peaceful here. Now we can talk.

ELLIDA: What about?

WANGEL: About you. And us. About our relationship. Ellida, we can't go on like this.

ELLIDA: What are you suggesting instead?

WANGEL: Complete trust between us. The kind of marriage we used to have.

ELLIDA: If only! But it can't be.

WANGEL: I understand. From certain things—I think I do understand.

ELLIDA: [*vehemently*] You don't! Don't say you understand!

WANGEL: Oh but I do. You're honest, Ellida. And faithful.

ELLIDA: Yes, I am.

WANGEL: To feel secure and happy, you must live in a full and open relationship.

ELLIDA: [*looking at him anxiously*] Yes. Go on.

WANGEL: You're not suited to be a man's second wife.

ELLIDA: Why do you say that now?

WANGEL: I've often had an inkling about it. But today, it struck me. The children's celebration … You saw me as a sort of accomplice. But no-one can erase their memories. I can't anyway.

ELLIDA: Yes, I know. How well I know.

WANGEL: But you're wrong. To you, it's almost as if the children's mother is still alive. As if she's an invisible presence among us. You feel that I've divided myself equally between you and her. So you see something almost immoral in our relationship. That's why you no longer can—or want to—live with me as my wife.

> ELLIDA *stands.*

ELLIDA: You've seen all this? Seen it all?

WANGEL: Yes, today I have—finally seen it. Down to the very depths.

ELLIDA: Down to the depths. No you haven't, believe me.

WANGEL: [*rising*] I know perfectly well there's more to it, Ellida.

ELLIDA: [*anxiously*] What do you know?

WANGEL: You can't thrive in these surroundings. The mountains weigh down on you and oppress you. There's not enough light for you here. Not enough open sky surrounding you. Not enough bracing power in the wind and the air.

ELLIDA: You're right, I am homesick. Night and day, winter and summer, I'm filled with this restless longing for the ocean.

WANGEL: I know, my dear Ellida. [*He puts his hand on her head.*] That's why I'll take my poor sick child back to her true home.

ELLIDA: What do you mean?

WANGEL: It's simple. We move.

ELLIDA: Move?!

WANGEL: Yes, somewhere out by the open sea. Somewhere you can find a home where you belong. A place that suits your spirit.

ELLIDA: Oh my dear, that's impossible. You mustn't even think of it! You wouldn't be happy anywhere else but here.

WANGEL: Do you think I can be happy here, without you?

ELLIDA: But I am here. And I'll stay here. You're not without me.

WANGEL: Aren't I, Ellida?

ELLIDA: We won't talk about it again. Everything you live and breathe for is here. Your life's work is here.

WANGEL: As I said, it can't be helped. We're going to move from this place. Move out there somewhere. And that's settled.

ELLIDA: What do you think will be gained by that?

WANGEL: You'll get back your health, your peace of mind.

ELLIDA: And what about you? What will you gain?

WANGEL: I'll win you back, my dearest.

ELLIDA: But you won't! You can't! That's what's so terrible. So dreadful to think about.

WANGEL: We'll see. If you keep having thoughts like that, clearly there's no other solution than to leave here. The sooner the better.

ELLIDA *makes a gesture.*

Yes Ellida, that's settled.

ELLIDA: No! That means I have to tell you the full truth. The way things are.

WANGEL: Yes you must.

ELLIDA: Come here and sit with me.

*They sit on the rock.*

The day you came out there and asked me if I wanted to belong to you, you spoke so openly and honestly about your first marriage. It had been so happy, you said.

WANGEL: And it was.

ELLIDA: I'm sure it was. I just want to remind you that I, too, was honest with you. I told you, openly, that at one time in my life I had loved someone else. That we had become engaged. In a way.

WANGEL: In a way?

ELLIDA: Something like that. He left. Later I broke it off. I told you all that.

WANGEL: But dear Ellida, why bring it up again? It didn't really concern me. And I've never even asked you who it was.

ELLIDA: No. You're always so kind and considerate.

WANGEL: [*smiling*] Oh well, in this case I could name him myself.

ELLIDA: You could name him?

WANGEL: Out there in Skjoldviken, there weren't many to choose from. Or rather, there was only one who—

ELLIDA: You're suggesting it was—Arnholm?

WANGEL: Of course. Wasn't it?

ELLIDA: No.

WANGEL: I don't understand—

ELLIDA: Do you remember the big American ship that came into Skjoldviken late one autumn for repairs?

WANGEL: I certainly do. They found the captain murdered in his cabin one morning. I went out and did the post-mortem myself.

ELLIDA: Yes, you did.

WANGEL: The second mate was supposed to have been the killer.

ELLIDA: Nobody could prove it!

WANGEL: Still, there was no doubt about it. Why else would he have drowned himself?

ELLIDA: He didn't drown himself. He went north on a ship.

WANGEL: [*surprised*] How do you know?

ELLIDA: [*with conviction*] I know because he was the man I was engaged to.

WANGEL: [*standing up, quickly*] What? This isn't possible!

ELLIDA: Yes, it was him.

WANGEL: But my God, Ellida! How on earth could you go and get engaged to a man like him? A complete stranger!

ELLIDA: He called himself Freeman. But later the letters he wrote were signed Alfred Johnston.

WANGEL: And where was he from?

ELLIDA: From Finnmark, he told me. But he was born in Finland.

WANGEL: A Finn. What else do you know about him?

ELLIDA: Just that he went to sea as a young boy. And that he'd travelled widely.

WANGEL: Nothing else?

ELLIDA: No. We mostly talked about the ocean.

WANGEL: Ah. The ocean.

ELLIDA: About storms and calms. Dark nights on the ocean. And the sea sparkling in the sunshine. But mostly we talked about the whales, the leaping dolphins, and the seals that lie out there on the rocks in the midday heat. We also talked about the gulls and sea eagles and all the other sea birds— And when we talked about things like that it seemed to me that he was of the same blood as all the creatures and birds of the sea.

WANGEL: And you?

ELLIDA: Yes. I almost felt I was one of them too.

WANGEL: I see. And then you got engaged to him?

ELLIDA: Yes. He told me I should.

WANGEL: Didn't you have a will of your own?

ELLIDA: Not when he was around. Afterwards, the whole thing felt … well, unfathomable.

WANGEL: Did you meet him often?

ELLIDA: Not very often. One day he came out to our place to have a look around the lighthouse. That's how I got to know him. Later we'd meet now and then. But when that business with the captain happened, he had to leave.

WANGEL: What do you know about that?

ELLIDA: Early one morning, at dawn, I had a note from him. It asked me to meet him at Bratthammeren. Out at the headland. I should go out there immediately, because he had to talk to me.

WANGEL: And you went?

ELLIDA: What else could I do. It was there he told me he had stabbed the captain during the night.

WANGEL: He admitted it!

ELLIDA: Yes, but he said he had only done what was right and proper.

WANGEL: But—did he say why?

ELLIDA: He said it didn't concern me.

WANGEL: And you just took his word for it?

ELLIDA: Yes. It never occurred to me not to. But just as he was about to say goodbye— No, you couldn't imagine what he did.

WANGEL: Tell me!

ELLIDA: He took a key-chain from his pocket and pulled a ring he always wore from his finger. Then he took a small ring I always wore from my finger, and put the two together on the chain. He said, now we are wedded to the open sea. And with those words, he threw the rings, with all his strength, as far as he could into the deep.

WANGEL: And you, Ellida, did you agree to it?

ELLIDA: Yes. It seemed the most natural thing in the world at the time. But then—thank God!—then he went away.

WANGEL: And after he'd gone?

ELLIDA: Oh I came to my senses again afterwards. I realised how reckless and ridiculous it had all been.

WANGEL: But you've heard from him since?

ELLIDA: He wrote to me from Archangel. He said he wanted to get across to America. And he told me where I could write to him.

WANGEL: And did you?

ELLIDA: Immediately. I told him that everything was over between us. That he should never think of me again, just as I would never think of him.

WANGEL: But he still wrote?

ELLIDA: Yes.

WANGEL: How did he react?

ELLIDA: It was as if I hadn't written. As if I hadn't broken it off. He wrote calmly and firmly that I should wait for him. He'd let me know when he was ready for me. And then I had to come to him at once.

WANGEL: So he still wouldn't let you go?

ELLIDA: No. So I wrote again. Almost word for word the same as the first. Stronger even.

WANGEL: But he didn't give up?

ELLIDA: No. He wrote back, as calm as before. I realised then that it was pointless. So I never wrote to him again.

WANGEL: And you never heard from him either?

ELLIDA: Yes, I've had three letters since then. Once he wrote from California, the second time from China. The last letter I had was from Australia. He was going to the goldfields.

WANGEL: That man must've had extraordinary powers over you, Ellida.

ELLIDA: Yes, yes. That dreadful man!

WANGEL: But you have to stop thinking about him. Never again! Promise me that, darling Ellida, please. Let's try to find a different cure. Fresher air than the air we breathe in the fjords. The sweeping, salty ocean air!

ELLIDA: Please don't! You mustn't even think of it. It wouldn't help. I couldn't shake it off anyway. That unfathomable power over my mind.

WANGEL: But you have shaken it off. When you broke it off with him. It's over.

ELLIDA: [*rising quickly*] But it isn't over! And it never will be. Not as long as I live!

WANGEL: [*in a stifled voice*] Do you mean that deep down, you'll never be able to forget this stranger?

ELLIDA: I did forget him. But suddenly he seemed to come back.

WANGEL: When was this?

ELLIDA: About three years ago. A little more, when I was carrying our child.

WANGEL: Ah! I see. [*He looks at her with pain*] To think that you've carried this love for another man these last three years. Not for me. Another.

ELLIDA: No! You're so wrong. All the love I carry is for you.

WANGEL: Then why have you refused to live with me as my wife all this time?

ELLIDA: Because of this fear the stranger provokes. A fear so deep and dreadful that it can only come from the depths of the ocean. And now—

*The young townspeople come back from the left, bow and go out again, right. With them are* ARNHOLM, BOLETTE, HILDE *and* LYNGSTRAND.

BOLETTE: [*as they pass*] Well well, you two are still up here!

ELLIDA: Yes, it's so nice and cool up here in the hills.

ARNHOLM: We're off to the dance.

WANGEL: Good, good. We'll be down soon, too.

HILDE: See you later, then!

ELLIDA: Oh, Mr Lyngstrand—could you wait a moment?

LYNGSTRAND *stops. The other three go out, right.*

[*To* LYNGSTRAND] Are you going dancing as well?

LYNGSTRAND: No, Mrs Wangel, I don't think I dare.

ELLIDA: No, it's best to be careful. With this chest of yours.

LYNGSTRAND: True enough.

ELLIDA: How long is it now, since you made that voyage you talked about earlier today?

LYNGSTRAND: Oh, I guess about … yes, it's about three years now.

ELLIDA: Three years.

LYNGSTRAND: Or a bit more.

ELLIDA: [*looking at* WANGEL] You see …?

WANGEL: But Ellida, my dear—

ELLIDA: Don't let us keep you, Mr Lyngstrand, go and join the others. But no dancing!

LYNGSTRAND: Only watching.

*He exits, right.*

ELLIDA: Johnston was on that ship.

WANGEL: What makes you think that?

ELLIDA: [*without answering him*] That's where he learnt that I had married someone else while he was away. And it was then, at that moment, that this fear came over me! And now at any time, I can suddenly see him, large as life, in front of me. Or rather, a little to the side. He never looks at me. He's just—there. Looking exactly the way I saw him last.

WANGEL: Ten years ago?

ELLIDA: Out on Bratthammeren. What I see clearest is his brooch, with its large, blue pearl, like the dead eye of a fish, and it seems to stare into me.

WANGEL: Dear God. You're sicker than I thought. Sicker than you know.

ELLIDA: Help me, Wangel, help me! I feel it's closing in all around me.

WANGEL: And you've been like this for three whole years. Carried this secret suffering inside you, without confiding in me.

ELLIDA: How could I? If I'd confided all this to you, I'd also have had to tell you something—something unspeakable.

WANGEL: Unspeakable?

ELLIDA: [*warding him off*] No, no! Don't ask! Just one more thing, and that's the end of it. Wangel—how can we solve this enigma with the child's eyes?

WANGEL: My dearest Ellida, I've told you, it's only in your imagination. Our child had exactly the same eyes as all children.

ELLIDA: No, he did not! His eyes changed colour with the sea. When the fjord was calm and sunny, so were his eyes. And they changed in stormy weather too. I saw it so clearly.

WANGEL: [*humouring her*] Alright. But even if they did?

ELLIDA: [*closer, in a low voice*] I have seen such eyes before.

WANGEL: When? Where?

ELLIDA: Out on Bratthammeren. Ten years ago.

    WANGEL *takes a step back.*

ELLIDA: [*whispering, trembling*] Our child had the eyes of the stranger.

WANGEL: [*crying out involuntarily*] Ellida!

ELLIDA: Now you must understand how I could never, don't ever dare to, live with you again as your wife.

    *She turns quickly and runs down the hill, right.* WANGEL *runs after her, calling:*

WANGEL: Ellida! Ellida! My poor unhappy Ellida!

# ACT THREE

*A secluded corner of* DR WANGEL'*s garden. The place is damp and marshy and overshadowed by large old trees. On the right is the edge of a stagnant pond. A low, open fence divides the garden from the path and the fjord beyond. In the far distance, across the fjord, mountain ranges and peaks can be seen.*

*It is late afternoon, early evening.* BOLETTE *is sitting on a stone bench, left, sewing. A few books and a sewing basket are lying on the bench.*

HILDE *and* LYNGSTRAND, *both with fishing rods and tackle, are walking along the edge of the pond.*

HILDE: [*making a sign to* LYNGSTRAND] Stop! I can see a big one.

LYNGSTRAND: Where?

HILDE: [*pointing*] Down there! And look! There's another one! [*Looking at the trees*] Oh no, look who's coming! He'll frighten them away.

BOLETTE: Who's coming?

HILDE: Your old teacher, that's who.

BOLETTE: My—?

ARNHOLM *appears through the trees, right.*

ARNHOLM: Any fish in the pond?

HILDE: Some very old carp.

ARNHOLM: So the old carp are still alive?

HILDE: They're tough old things. But we'll soon get the better of them.

ARNHOLM: Why not try out on the fjord?

LYNGSTRAND: No, has to be the pond. It's more mysterious, sort of.

HILDE: Yes, it's more exciting here. Have you been swimming?

ARNHOLM: I came straight here from the bathing hut.

HILDE: You stayed close to the shore?

ARNHOLM: I'm not a strong swimmer.

HILDE: Can you do backstroke?

ARNHOLM: No.

HILDE: I can. [*To* LYNGSTRAND] Let's try on the other side.

*They walk along the edge of the pond and exit right.*

ARNHOLM: [*joining* BOLETTE] You're sitting here, all by yourself?

BOLETTE: Yes. I do most of the time.

ARNHOLM: Your mother isn't down in the garden?

BOLETTE: She's out walking with Father.

ARNHOLM: How is she?

BOLETTE: I forgot to ask.

ARNHOLM: What are those books you have there?

BOLETTE: Oh, one is about plants. The other about geography.

ARNHOLM: You like reading things like that?

BOLETTE: When I can find the time. First of all I have to see to the housework.

ARNHOLM: But surely your mother—stepmother—doesn't she help with that?

BOLETTE: No, that's my job. I had to do it for two years when father was alone. And then—well it just stayed like that.

ARNHOLM: Good to see you're still fond of reading.

BOLETTE: I read anything I can lay my hands on. We're so isolated here, outside of the mainstream. Well, almost.

ARNHOLM: Why do you say that, Bolette?

BOLETTE: Because it's true. I don't think our lives are much different from the carp's down there in the pond. They have the fjord so close, where the big shoals of wild fish rush in and out. But the poor, tame domesticated fish never get to know that. They can never get out there and be a part of it all.

ARNHOLM: But I doubt it'd suit them.

    *Pause.*

Besides, you can't say that life passes you by here. Not in summer, at least, when the town almost becomes an international meeting place. A sort of cosmopolitan crossroads.

BOLETTE: [*smiling*] It's easy for you to make fun of us, as you're passing through.

ARNHOLM: I make fun—?

BOLETTE: Crossroads, cosmopolitan life … that's what the town people like to say. But what do we gain from the great outside world passing through on its way to the midnight sun? We're stuck here. No midnight sun for us, we have to go on living here in our fish pond.

ARNHOLM: [*sitting down beside her*] Dear Bolette, please tell me if there's something—or perhaps one thing in particular—you keep longing for?

BOLETTE: What I long for most of all is to be let out.

ARNHOLM: More than anything else?

BOLETTE: Yes. And then, to be able to learn more. To know about things. All sorts of things.

ARNHOLM: When I was your teacher, your father often said that you'd be allowed to study.

BOLETTE: Ah—poor Father. He says so many things. But when it comes to the crunch, I'm afraid he hasn't got much initiative.

ARNHOLM: Well yes. But have you talked to him about it? I mean, seriously discussed it?

BOLETTE: No. I suppose there isn't a lot of initiative in me either.

ARNHOLM: Hm. Don't you think you're being rather unfair to yourself?

BOLETTE: Am I? Besides, Father has other things on his mind than thinking about me and my future. He doesn't really want to either, being worried about Ellida.

ARNHOLM: How's that?

BOLETTE: He and my stepmother [*She breaks off.*] … Father and Mother have their own lives to live.

ARNHOLM: I see. So much the better if you could get away from here.

BOLETTE: Yes, you're right. I should think about myself as well. Look for some position or other. Once Father's gone, I'll have no-one— But poor Father, I'd worry about leaving him.

ARNHOLM: He'll still have your stepmother.

BOLETTE: Yes. But she's not suited to doing all the things our mother did. There's so much she just doesn't see. Or perhaps doesn't want to see. Or doesn't care about. I don't know which it is.

ARNHOLM: I think I understand.

BOLETTE: Poor Father. He's quite weak in some ways. He doesn't have enough work to keep him busy either. And she just isn't capable of helping him. But then, of course, that's partly his own fault.

ARNHOLM: How?

BOLETTE: Father always wants to be surrounded by happy faces. Fill the house with sunshine and happiness. I'm afraid that's why he often lets her have medicines that can't be good for her in the long run.

ARNHOLM: Do you really believe that?

BOLETTE: Perhaps I'm imagining it. But she's so—peculiar at times. [*Impetuously*] But it's unfair, isn't it, that I have to live here at home? And don't I have a duty to myself as well? But I suspect I was created to remain here in the pond with old Father Carp.

ARNHOLM: No you weren't. But it's up to you.

BOLETTE: Do you mean that?

ARNHOLM: [*lively*] Believe you me. It's all in your own hands.

BOLETTE: Oh, if only—! I wonder … would you, could you, have a word with Father?

ARNHOLM: I will. But first, I've something I want to talk to you about, Bolette. [*Looks left*] Oh. We'll talk about it later.

> ELLIDA *enters. She is hatless, wearing a large shawl over her head and shoulders.*

ELLIDA: [*restlessly, animated*] Oh yes, it's good to be here! It's so lovely here!

ARNHOLM: [*standing up*] Nice walk?

ELLIDA: Yes, a long, glorious walk in the hills. With Wangel. And now we're going sailing.

BOLETTE: Won't you sit down?

ELLIDA: No, thank you. I won't sit.

BOLETTE: [*moving to make room*] There's plenty of room.

ELLIDA: [*walking around*] No, no, no. I won't sit. Won't sit.

ARNHOLM: That walk seems to have agreed with you. You look revived.

ELLIDA: Oh I feel so well! So incredibly happy! So safe! So very safe … [*She looks out, left*] What's that big ship coming in?

BOLETTE: [*standing up*] It must be the big English one.

ARNHOLM: Does it usually stop here?

BOLETTE: Only for about half an hour. Then it goes further up the fjord.

ELLIDA: And then out again, tomorrow. Out on the great open sea. Just imagine—to be let out, to be on board!

ARNHOLM: Have you ever been on a long sea voyage, Mrs Wangel?

ELLIDA: No. Never. Only short trips here in the fjords.

BOLETTE: Alas. We have to be content with dry land.

ARNHOLM: Well, it is our natural element.

ELLIDA: I don't believe that at all.

ARNHOLM: That land is our natural element?

ELLIDA: I think if the human race had learnt to live on the ocean, even in the ocean, from the beginning, we'd have reached a different perfection by now. Both better and happier.

ARNHOLM: You really believe that?

ELLIDA: I wonder if we wouldn't have. I've often talked to Wangel about it …

ARNHOLM: And he—?

ELLIDA: He thinks I may be right.

ARNHOLM: [*jokingly*] Well why not! But what's passed is past. We took the wrong turning and became land creatures instead of ocean creatures. It's too late to correct the mistake.

ELLIDA: And that's the sad truth of it. And I think we land creatures sense it, that we carry it within us as a secret regret, even sorrow. Believe me, there lies the deepest spring of human melancholy.

ARNHOLM: I believe people live their lives quite happily.

ELLIDA: That kind of happiness is merely a reflection of the long, light summer days. A reminder of the dark days ahead. There was the fjord, bright and blue. And then, suddenly—

BOLETTE: You shouldn't give in to such sad thoughts. You were so cheerful and lively just now.

ELLIDA: Yes, I was. Wasn't I. Oh all this … it's so silly of me. If only Wangel could come. He promised me. Yet he doesn't come. He must have forgotten. Mr Arnholm, could you go and find him for me?

ARNHOLM: Yes, of course.

ELLIDA: Tell him he must come at once. Because now I can't see him—

ARNHOLM: Can't see him?

ELLIDA: You wouldn't understand. When he's not here, I sometimes can't remember what he looks like. And then it's as if I've lost him. It's so painful! Please hurry!

*She walks up and down beside the pond.*

BOLETTE: [*to* ARNHOLM] I'll come with you. You wouldn't know—

ARNHOLM: Oh, I'm sure I'll—

BOLETTE: [*low voice*] I'm worried. Afraid he'll be on board the steamer.

ARNHOLM: Afraid?

BOLETTE: He usually goes on board to see if he knows anyone. And they serve … refreshments, and—

ARNHOLM: Ah. Let's go.

ARNHOLM *and* BOLETTE *go out, left.*

ELLIDA *stands for a while, gazing into the pond. Now and then she mutters quietly to herself.*

*Along the footpath beyond the garden fence a* STRANGER *enters from the left. He has bushy, reddish hair and beard. He's wearing a 'Scottish' cap, with a travelling bag slung over his shoulder.*

*The stranger walks along the fence and looks into the garden. When he sees* ELLIDA, *he stops, looks fixedly and searchingly at her, then says softly:*

STRANGER: Good evening, Ellida.

ELLIDA: [*turning and calling out*] Finally, there you are, my dear!

STRANGER: Yes. Finally.

ELLIDA: [*staring at him in surprise, apprehensively*] Who are you? Are you looking for someone?

STRANGER: You know I am, Ellida.

ELLIDA: [*startled*] You know my name? Who are you looking for?

STRANGER: For you, of course.

ELLIDA: [*shivering*] Ah!

*She stares at him. Staggers back with a half-choked cry.*

The eyes! The eyes!

STRANGER: Do you finally recognise me? I knew you immediately, Ellida.

ELLIDA: The eyes! Don't look at me like that! I'll call for help!

STRANGER: Shh. Don't be afraid. You know I don't mean any harm.

ELLIDA: [*covering her eyes*] I told you, don't look at me like that!

STRANGER: [*leaning on the fence*] I came on the English steamer.

ELLIDA: [*looking at him timidly*] What do you want with me?

STRANGER: I promised I'd come back as soon as I could —

ELLIDA: Go away! Go! Never come back, never! I wrote to you that it had to be over between us. Everything. You know that!

STRANGER: [*unperturbed*] I would've liked to have come to you earlier. But I couldn't. Finally, I was able to. So here you have me again, Ellida.

ELLIDA: What do you want with me? Why are you here?

STRANGER: I've come to fetch you, Ellida. You know I have.

ELLIDA: [*recoiling anxiously*] To fetch me! Is that your intention?

STRANGER: Yes, of course it is.

ELLIDA: But don't you know that I'm married?

STRANGER: Yes, I know.

ELLIDA: Yet you still—! You've still come to fetch me!

STRANGER: I have, yes.

ELLIDA: [*holding her hands to her head*] Oh, this is horrible! Dreadful, dreadful …

STRANGER: Don't you want to?

ELLIDA: No no no! I don't want to! I cannot. I will not. [*More calmly*] And I dare not.

STRANGER: [*climbing the fence into the garden*] Alright, Ellida, alright. Let me say just one more thing before I leave.

> ELLIDA *tries to run away, but can't. She stands as though paralysed by fear, supporting herself on the tree stump by the pond.*

ELLIDA: Don't touch me! Don't come near me. No closer.

STRANGER: [*walking cautiously towards her*] Don't be afraid of me, Ellida.

ELLIDA: [*holding her hands over her eyes*] Don't look at me like that!

STRANGER: Don't be afraid. Not afraid.

WANGEL *comes through the garden from the left.*

WANGEL: [*still among the trees*] Well, I've certainly kept you waiting.

ELLIDA *rushes towards him, clings to his arm and cries.*

ELLIDA: Oh Wangel, save me! You must save me. Can you save me?

WANGEL: Ellida! What in God's name?

ELLIDA: Don't you see him? There! He's standing over there!

WANGEL *looks at the* STRANGER *and approaches him.*

WANGEL: Excuse me, who are you? And what are you doing in our garden?

STRANGER: [*indicating* ELLIDA *with a nod*] I've come to talk to her.

WANGEL: What do you want with my wife? Do you know him, Ellida?

ELLIDA: [*low voice, wringing her hands*] Do I know him! Yes. It's him, Wangel! It's him!

WANGEL: [*turning to the* STRANGER] Are you the Johnston who—?

STRANGER: You can call me Johnston, I don't mind. But that's not my name. Not anymore.

WANGEL: What do you want with my wife? I'm sure you know that the lighthouse-keeper's daughter, as you knew her, was married a long time ago.

STRANGER: I've known for over three years.

ELLIDA: [*tensely*] How did you find out?

STRANGER: I was on my way home to you when I read about your wedding.

ELLIDA *stares fixedly ahead.*

I was aggravated. Because those rings ... that was a kind of wedding too, Ellida.

ELLIDA: Oh ...

WANGEL: How dare you!

STRANGER: Had you forgotten?

ELLIDA: [*covering her face*] Don't look at me like that!

WANGEL: [*placing himself between them*] Address yourself to me, not to her. And since you are aware of the circumstances, what are you really doing here?

STRANGER: I promised Ellida to come to her as soon as I could.

WANGEL: Ellida! You keep calling her Ellida!

STRANGER: Ellida had promised me faithfully to wait until I came.

WANGEL: Stop addressing my wife by her first name.

STRANGER: As she still belongs to me, first of all—

ELLIDA *moves behind* WANGEL.

ELLIDA: Ah! He'll never let me go!

WANGEL: You say she belongs to you!

STRANGER: Has she told you about the two rings? Mine and hers?

WANGEL: Yes. But that's in the past. Finished. She wrote to you.

STRANGER: Ellida and I agreed that those rings would bind us together. .

ELLIDA: But I don't want to! I don't want to have anything to do with you ever again. Don't look at me like that!

WANGEL: You must be out of your mind if you think you can come here and claim such rights to what was nothing but childish nonsense.

STRANGER: No, I don't have any 'rights' as you call them.

WANGEL: So what do you intend? To take her from me by force? Against her will?

STRANGER: What use would that be? If Ellida wants to be with me, she has to leave here of her own free will.

ELLIDA: [*startled*] Free will!

WANGEL: Surely you don't imagine that—

ELLIDA: [*to herself*] My own free will.

WANGEL: You must be mad. Please leave. We don't want to have anything more to do with you.

STRANGER: [*looking at his watch*] It's almost time for me to board again. [*Takes a step towards* ELLIDA] Well, Ellida. I have fulfilled my part of the pledge. [*Moves closer*] I've kept my promise.

ELLIDA: [*pleadingly, as she moves away*] Please, don't touch me!

STRANGER: You have until tomorrow night to think it over—

WANGEL: There's nothing to think over. Now get out!

STRANGER: I'm going with the steamer up into the fjord. And tomorrow night I'll be back here again. Wait for me here in the garden.

ELLIDA: [*imploring*] No, no! Don't come tomorrow night! Don't come here ever again!

STRANGER: If you decide to come with me, out across the ocean—

ELLIDA: Please, don't look at me like that!

STRANGER: You have to be prepared for the journey.

WANGEL: Go into the house, Ellida.

ELLIDA: I can't! Help me! Save me, Wangel!

STRANGER: Remember this—if you don't come with me tomorrow, everything's finished.

ELLIDA: [*looking at him, trembling*] Everything? Forever?

STRANGER: [*nodding*] I'll never return. You'll never see me again. Nor hear from me. It'll be as if I were dead and gone. Lost to you forever.

ELLIDA: [*catching her breath*] Ah—!

STRANGER: So think carefully about what you decide. Goodbye! [*He walks to the fence, climbs over and turns*] Yes, Ellida, be prepared for the journey tomorrow night. I will be here to fetch you.

> *He walks slowly, calmly, down the path, right.* ELLIDA *stands for some time, watching him leave.*

ELLIDA: Of my own free will, he said. Imagine—he said I should come with him of my own free will.

WANGEL: Just stay calm. He's gone now. And you'll never see him again.

ELLIDA: [*thoughtfully, not listening to him*] When he has been here, tomorrow night? And when he has left on the steamer across the seas?

WANGEL: Yes?

ELLIDA: I wonder, will he ever come back?

WANGEL: Ellida. You can rest assured he won't. What could he possibly want here, now that he has heard from your own lips that you want nothing to do with him?

ELLIDA: [*to herself*] Tomorrow then. Or never.

WANGEL: And if he should even think of coming here again—

ELLIDA: Yes? What then?

WANGEL: We have the power to stop him. If you can't get any peace from him in any other way, we'll make him pay for the murder of the captain.

ELLIDA: [*vehemently*] No, no! Never that! We don't know anything about the captain's murder.

WANGEL: We do! He confessed it to you!

ELLIDA: No. I'll deny it. Don't lock him up. He belongs out on the open sea. He belongs out there.

WANGEL: [*looking at her, he speaks slowly*] Oh Ellida. Ellida!

ELLIDA: [*clinging to him passionately*] My dearest husband—save me from that man!

WANGEL: [*gently freeing himself*] Come! Come with me!

LYNGSTRAND *and* HILDE *, both with fishing tackle, enter by the pond, right.* LYNGSTRAND *walks quickly to* ELLIDA.

LYNGSTRAND: Mrs Wangel! I've got some very strange news for you. Imagine! We've seen the American!

HILDE: We both saw him.

LYNGSTRAND: He came out from the back garden and then boarded the big English steamer. I went to sea with him once. I was sure he'd drowned. But here he is, large as life! I'm pretty sure he has come to revenge himself on his unfaithful wife.

WANGEL: What did you say?

HILDE: Lyngstrand's going to use him to create a work of art.

WANGEL: I don't understand a word of—

ELLIDA: I'll explain later.

ARNHOLM *and* BOLETTE *enter by the path outside the fence, left.*

BOLETTE: Come and look! The English steamer's going up the fjord.

*A large ship glides slowly past in the distance.*

LYNGSTRAND: [*to* HILDE ] I'm sure he'll find her tonight.

HILDE: Yes! The seaman's unfaithful wife.

LYNGSTRAND: And imagine! Right on midnight.

HILDE: It'll be so inspiring.

ELLIDA: [*looking after the ship*] Tomorrow then …

WANGEL: And then never again.

ELLIDA: [*low, trembling voice*] Oh Wangel—save me from myself!

WANGEL: [*anxiously*] Ellida!

ELLIDA: That man is like the open sea.

*She walks slowly and pensively through the garden and out, left.* WANGEL *walks uneasily beside her, watching her closely.*

# ACT FOUR

*Dr Wangel's garden room. Doors right and left. In the background, between two windows, an open door leads onto the verandah. Beyond we see part of the garden. Down left, a sofa and table. Right, a piano, and further back a large flower stand. Centre of the room is a round table with chairs. On the table is a flowering rose and other pot plants. It is morning.*

BOLETTE *is sitting on the sofa by the table, left, embroidering.* LYNGSTRAND *is sitting on a chair at the top end of the table, his arms resting on the table. He sits silently for a moment, watching* BOLETTE. BALLESTED, *down in the garden, is sitting painting.* HILDE *watches him working.*

LYNGSTRAND: It must be pretty difficult, Miss Wangel, to embroider that kind of pattern.

BOLETTE: It's not so difficult if you take care with the counting.

LYNGSTRAND: Counting? You have to count as well?

BOLETTE: Yes, the stitches. Look.

LYNGSTRAND: Fancy that. It's almost like a form of art. Can you draw, too?

BOLETTE: Oh yes, when I have a pattern to copy.

LYNGSTRAND: So it's not real art after all.

BOLETTE: No, it's more like a sort of handicraft.

LYNGSTRAND: All the same, perhaps you could learn to be an artist.

BOLETTE: Even when I don't have any talent?

LYNGSTRAND: Even then. If you could be with a genuine artist all the time …

BOLETTE: You think he could teach me?

LYNGSTRAND: Not exactly teach. But inspire you, little by little. It might work wonders, like a miracle.

BOLETTE: A little miracle. How odd.

LYNGSTRAND: [*after a moment*] Have you ever thought much—? I mean thought seriously, about marriage, Miss Wangel?

BOLETTE: [*glancing quickly at him*] Marriage—? No.

LYNGSTRAND: I have.

BOLETTE: You have?

LYNGSTRAND: Yes. I often think about things. Mostly about marriage. I think marriage must be considered as a sort of wonder. The way a woman is gradually transformed into becoming like her husband.

BOLETTE: Do you believe that the things a man has studied, or has decided to dedicate his life to, can be passed on to his wife?

LYNGSTRAND: Oh yes, they can. Little by little. As if by some sort of miracle. But I know, too, that it can only happen in a truly happy marriage, based on love and devotion.

BOLETTE: Has it ever occurred to you that a man might be influenced by his wife in the same way?

LYNGSTRAND: A man. No never.

BOLETTE: But if a woman, why not a man?

LYNGSTRAND: A man has a vocation, something to strive for. That's what gives a man strength and purpose.

BOLETTE: All men?

LYNGSTRAND: No, I'm really thinking about artists.

BOLETTE: Do you think it's right for an artist to get married? Shouldn't he live for his art?

LYNGSTRAND: Of course he must. But he can do that just as easily even if he's married.

BOLETTE: But what about her?

LYNGSTRAND: Her?

BOLETTE: The woman he marries. What's she going to live for?

LYNGSTRAND: She too must live for his art. Surely that would give a woman a great sense of happiness.

BOLETTE: I wouldn't bet on it …

LYNGSTRAND: Oh yes, Miss Wangel. It's not just the honour and recognition she enjoys because of him but the fact that she's allowed to ease the work for him, taking care of him, making his life nice and pleasant. Surely that's a wonderful duty for a woman.

BOLETTE: You've no idea how selfish you sound!

LYNGSTRAND: Me? Selfish? Good God! If only you knew me a little better. [*Leans closer to her*] Miss Wangel, when I'm gone—and it won't be long now —

BOLETTE: [*looking compassionately at him*] No need for such sad thoughts.

LYNGSTRAND: Oh, I wouldn't call them sad. I'm leaving in about a month's time. I'm off to the south. To the Mediterranean.

BOLETTE: Oh. Yes. Of course.

LYNGSTRAND: Will you think about me now and then, Miss Wangel?

BOLETTE: Yes of course I will.

LYNGSTRAND: [*happily*] Good! You promise?

BOLETTE: I promise.

LYNGSTRAND: Word of honour, Miss Bolette?

BOLETTE: Word of honour. [*Changes her mood*] But what is it all for? It won't lead to anything.

LYNGSTRAND: How can you say that? It will be wonderful for me to know you're sitting here at home, thinking of me.

BOLETTE: And then? After that?

LYNGSTRAND: After that? I haven't actually thought—

BOLETTE: There's so much in the way. Everything is in the way.

LYNGSTRAND: Some kind of miracle might happen.

BOLETTE: [*lively*] That's right, isn't it? You do believe that, don't you?

LYNGSTRAND: Oh yes I do. And then, in a few years, when I return home as a famous sculptor, prosperous and bursting with health—!

BOLETTE: Yes. Let's hope you do.

LYNGSTRAND: If you'll think of me faithfully and lovingly while I'm away. As you promised.

BOLETTE: Yes, as I promised. [*Shakes her head*] But it can never lead to anything, you know.

LYNGSTRAND: Yes, it can. At least, it'll allow me to work on my art so much easier and with more inspiration.

BOLETTE: And you believe that?

LYNGSTRAND: I can feel it inside. And I think it'd be inspiring for you, too, tucked away here in this backwater, to know that in your own way, you're helping me to create.

BOLETTE *looks at him, then:*

BOLETTE: Shh! Let's talk about something else. Here comes the headmaster.

ARNHOLM *appears in the garden, left. He stops and talks to* BALLESTED *and* HILDE .

LYNGSTRAND: Are you fond of your old teacher, Miss Bolette?

BOLETTE: Am I fond of—?

LYNGSTRAND: I mean, do you like him?

BOLETTE: Yes I do. He's a very good a friend and advisor.

LYNGSTRAND: Don't you think it's strange that he has never married?

BOLETTE: I suppose it hasn't been easy for him to find someone who'll have him. Most of the girls he knows have been his students.

LYNGSTRAND: What's wrong with that?

BOLETTE: Good God, you don't marry someone who's been your teacher!

LYNGSTRAND: Don't you think a girl can love her teacher?

BOLETTE: Not once she's grown up. Shh!

BALLESTED, *having collected equipment etc, carries it out through the garden, right.* HILDE *helps him.* ARNHOLM *comes up on the verandah and enters the garden room.*

ARNHOLM: Good morning, my dear Bolette. Good morning, Mr … Mr … Hm.

*He looks annoyed, nods coldly to* LYNGSTRAND, *who rises and bows.*

BOLETTE: [*standing and walking to* ARNHOLM] Good morning, Mr Arnholm.

ARNHOLM: And how are things today?

BOLETTE: Fine, thank you.

ARNHOLM: Is your mother down there swimming again?

BOLETTE: No, she's up in her room.

ARNHOLM: Not feeling well?

BOLETTE: I don't know. She has locked herself in.

ARNHOLM: Has she now?

LYNGSTRAND: It seems Mrs Wangel was very upset by that American yesterday. I told her I'd seen him, large as life!

BOLETTE: [*to* ARNHOLM] You and Father stayed up late last night.

ARNHOLM: We had something rather important to discuss.

BOLETTE: Did you get a chance to say something to him about me?

ARNHOLM: No, my dear Bolette. I didn't. He was very preoccupied with something else.

BOLETTE: [*sighing*] Oh well. He always is …

ARNHOLM: [*looking meaningly at her*] But we'll talk about it later.

DR WANGEL *comes in through the door, left.*

WANGEL: [*holding out his hand*] Here already, my dear friend? Kind of you to come so early. There's more I'd like to talk to you about.

BOLETTE: [*to* LYNGSTRAND] Why don't we go and join Hilde in the garden?

LYNGSTRAND: Yes, Miss Wangel, I'd love to.

LYNGSTRAND *and* BOLETTE *go into the garden and out through the trees.*

ARNHOLM: What do you think about that young man spending so much time with the girls?

WANGEL: I haven't noticed.

ARNHOLM: You ought to keep an eye on that sort of thing.

WANGEL: But what do you expect me to do? The girls are so used to looking after themselves, you can't tell them anything. Well, I can't—and as for Ellida—Besides, I can't ask her to play a role in such things. It's not for her to—[*breaks off*] However. Have you given it any more thought? What we spoke of?

ARNHOLM: I haven't thought of anything else.

*Pause,*

How is she today?

WANGEL: I was with her just now, and she seemed quite calm. But underneath all her moods, there's something hidden which I cannot get a grip on. And she's so changeable—so unpredictable, and erratic.

ARNHOLM: Surely that's a result of her morbid state of mind?

WANGEL: Not altogether. I believe it's something she was born with. Ellida belongs to the ocean people.

ARNHOLM: What do you mean, Wangel?

WANGEL: Haven't you noticed that people out there by the ocean are a law unto themselves? It's almost as if they lived the life of the ocean itself. Their thoughts and feelings ebb and flow. And they can never be resettled. I should've thought about it earlier. It was a sin to take Ellida away from the ocean and into the fjord!

ARNHOLM: Is that what you believe now?

WANGEL: Deep down I think I knew it then. But I didn't allow it to surface. I loved her so much, you see. So I put myself first. It was unforgivably selfish of me!

ARNHOLM: All men are a bit selfish in those circumstances.

WANGEL: [*restlessly pacing the room*] But I've just kept blindly going. And I'm so much older. Perhaps I should've been more like a father, guiding her. Helped to develop and mature her mind. But I never took the initiative! Because I wanted her—preferred her—the way she was. But when she got worse and worse, I simply didn't know what to do. [*Lowering his voice*] That's why I wrote and asked you to come.

ARNHOLM: [*Looking at him, amazed*] Was that why you wrote?

WANGEL: But I was on the wrong track. I thought Ellida had once been in love with you. That she secretly missed you. That it would do her good to see you again, talk with you about her home and the past.

ARNHOLM: So it was your wife you meant when you wrote that someone here was waiting for me and—perhaps even longing for me!

WANGEL: Who else?

ARNHOLM: No. No, you're right. I misunderstood …

WANGEL: As I said, I was on the wrong track. But I daren't reject any means that could possibly ease her mind a little.

ARNHOLM: How do you explain the strange power the American has over her?

WANGEL: Hm. Perhaps there are aspects of that which can never be explained.

ARNHOLM: But do you actually believe in something like that?

WANGEL: I neither believe nor disbelieve. I don't know.

ARNHOLM: But this strangely sinister claim that the child's eyes were—?

WANGEL: [*eagerly*] No, I don't believe all that about the eyes! I refuse to believe it! It exists purely in Ellida's imagination.

ARNHOLM: Did you notice the man's eyes when you saw him yesterday?

WANGEL: I certainly did.

ARNHOLM: And?

WANGEL: [*evasively*] But good heavens, what do you expect me to say. It wasn't even daylight when I saw him. And besides, Ellida had spoken so much about this similarity that—I really don't know what I saw.

ARNHOLM: But what about the other thing? That the fear and restlessness came over her just when this stranger was supposed to be on his way back?

WANGEL: That has to be something she's imagined as well. And in the last two days, it has become real to her. It didn't come over her suddenly, as she now claims. I noticed signs of it long before then. Admittedly, she did have a fairly severe attack three years ago. In March.

ARNHOLM: So after all …

WANGEL: Yes, but that can be explained quite simply by her condition at the time.

ARNHOLM: One thing versus another.

WANGEL: [*clasping his hands*] Being unable to help her. Not knowing which way to turn!

ARNHOLM: Suppose you could decide to move—go somewhere else? Where she could live in surroundings a bit more like home?

WANGEL: My dear Arnholm, don't you think I've already offered her! I even suggested we move to Skjoldviken. But she doesn't want to. Doesn't believe it'll be of any use. And she may well be right. Besides, I honestly don't know how I could manage it. How I could justify taking the girls out to such a backwater. They need to live where there's at least some prospects of them getting married.

ARNHOLM: So you are thinking about that?

WANGEL: Of course! But on the other hand there's my poor, sick Ellida … Oh, Arnholm, I seem to be caught between the devil and the deep blue sea!

ARNHOLM: I don't think you need to worry too much about Bolette—

[*Breaks off*] I wonder where she—where they've all gone?

ARNHOLM *goes to the door and looks out.* WANGEL *goes to the piano.*

WANGEL: I would gladly make any sacrifice, for all three of them. If I only knew how …

ELLIDA *enters by the door, left. She moves quickly to* WANGEL.

ELLIDA: Please, don't go anywhere this morning!

WANGEL: Of course I won't. [*Indicates* ARNHOLM] Don't you want to greet your friend?

ELLIDA: [*turning*] Mr Arnholm! [*Holding out her hand*] Good morning.

ARNHOLM: Good morning, Mrs Wangel. Not having your usual swim today?

ELLIDA: No, no no! Not today. Won't you sit down for a moment?

ARNHOLM: No, thank you. [*He looks across at* WANGEL] I promised the girls I'd join them down in the garden.

ELLIDA: God knows if you'll find them there. I never know where they get to.

WANGEL: They're usually somewhere around the pond.

ARNHOLM: I dare say I'll track them down.

ARNHOLM *nods, crosses the verandah and goes out through the garden, right.*

ELLIDA: What's the time, Wangel?

WANGEL: [*looking at his watch*] Just after eleven.

ELLIDA: Just after … at eleven, eleven thirty tonight, the steamship returns. If only it could be over.

WANGEL: There's something I'd like to ask you. You said that you've often seen him before you these last three years —

ELLIDA: Yes, I have.

WANGEL: What was he like when you saw him?

ELLIDA: You saw yourself what he looks like.

WANGEL: But in your mind's eye—in your projection of him?

ELLIDA: As I saw him last night, in real life.

WANGEL: Then why didn't you recognise him immediately?

ELLIDA: [*surprised*] You're right. That *is* odd, isn't it.

WANGEL: You said it was only the eyes—

ELLIDA: Yes, the eyes! The eyes!

WANGEL: But up on the lookout you said he always appeared to you the way he was when you parted, ten years ago.

ELLIDA: Then I suppose he must have looked the same then as he does now.

WANGEL: You gave me quite a different description of him that night. [*Looks closely at her*] Try to think. Perhaps you can no longer remember what he looked like when he threw the rings in the ocean?

ELLIDA: [*closing her eyes for a moment; thoughtfully*] Not clearly. Isn't that odd?

WANGEL: Not now that you've seen the man in the flesh. And that overshadows the old one.

ELLIDA: So that's what you think?

WANGEL: I do. And it overshadows your sick illusions, too. That's why I think it's a good thing that he has turned up.

ELLIDA: Good?

WANGEL: Yes. It may lead to your recovery.

ELLIDA: [*sitting on the sofa*] Wangel, come and sit here with me. I must share my thoughts with you now.

WANGEL: Please do, Ellida.

*He sits on a chair on the other side of the table.*

ELLIDA: It was a great misfortune, for both of us, that you and I ever met.

WANGEL: What are you saying?

ELLIDA: It's not surprising, considering the way we came together.

WANGEL: What was wrong with it?

ELLIDA: Now you must listen to me. It's no use keeping on lying to ourselves, and each other.

WANGEL: How are we lying?

ELLIDA: At least we're hiding the truth. And the truth, purely and simply, is that you came out there and—and bought me.

WANGEL: Bought! You believe I bought you?

ELLIDA: I wasn't the slightest bit better. I accepted. I sold myself to you.

WANGEL: [*looking at her in pain*] Ellida. How do you have the heart to call it that?

ELLIDA: Is there any other name for it? You couldn't carry the emptiness in your house any longer. You looked around for a new wife.

WANGEL: And a new mother for my children, yes.

ELLIDA: Yes, that too, among other things. Although you had no idea whether I was capable or even suitable for the roles. You had only seen me a few times, spoken to me briefly. Then you realised you wanted me.

WANGEL: Call it what you will.

ELLIDA: And I for my part, I stood there helpless, bewildered, feeling so alone. So of course I accepted when you offered to provide for me for the rest of my life.

WANGEL: Ellida, I never thought of it as 'providing' for you.

ELLIDA: Even so, I should never have accepted! Not at any price. Far better the poorest of circumstances, if they were of my own choice.

WANGEL: [*standing up*] So the five or six years we've lived together have counted for nothing at all?

ELLIDA: Please, you must never believe that! You've given me everything. But I never came to your home of my own free will. That's the only thing that counts.

WANGEL: Not—not of your own free will!

ELLIDA: No. I didn't leave with you of my own free will.

WANGEL: [*subdued*] Ah. The stranger's phrase.

ELLIDA: Everything lies in those words. I can see that now.

WANGEL: What do you see?

ELLIDA: That our life together is not a real marriage.

WANGEL: [*bitterly*] You've never said a truer word. The life we live now is no marriage.

ELLIDA: It never was. From the very beginning.

*She stares ahead, unseeing.*

The first one … that could have become a real marriage. Mine, to him.

WANGEL: I don't understand you!

ELLIDA: Let's stop lying to each other. We can never escape the fact that a promise given freely is just as binding as a marriage.

WANGEL: But what—!

ELLIDA: [*rising, in a strong voice*] I want to leave you, Wangel. Please, let me go!

WANGEL: Ellida! Oh Ellida?

ELLIDA: That's all I ask. Believe me, it will lead to that anyway. Because of the way we came together.

WANGEL: [*controlling his pain*] So this is what it has come to?

ELLIDA: This is what it had to come to.

WANGEL: [*looking sadly at her*] So I've never owned you fully in all these years we've had together.

ELLIDA: Oh, Wangel, if only I could love you the way I want to. As deeply as you deserve! But I can't. It'll never happen.

WANGEL: Divorce, then? Is it divorce you want? Full, legal divorce?

ELLIDA: Oh my dear, you don't understand. I don't care about the formalities. I want us, you and I, to agree to release each other of our own free will.

WANGEL: [*bitterly, nodding slowly*] Break the deal we made. I see.

ELLIDA: Exactly! Break the deal.

WANGEL: And afterwards? Have you thought about what it's going to be like for both of us? How life will turn out for us?

ELLIDA: I don't worry about the future, what it will bring. The most important thing is that you set me free. I beg you, Wangel, implore you. Give me back my freedom.

WANGEL: Ellida, you are asking a terrible thing of me. Let's talk about it some more. At least give me time to resolve it. Give yourself time to consider everything.

ELLIDA: But there is no time. I must have my freedom today!

*Pause.*

Because he comes tonight. I have to be completely free when I face him. I don't want to hide behind that fact that I'm another man's wife. The choice has to be mine. Whether to let him go. Or to go with him.

WANGEL: Are you aware of what you're saying? Go with him! Place your whole future in his hands!

ELLIDA: But I placed my whole future in your hands, didn't I?

WANGEL: But him? A total stranger! You know almost nothing about him.

ELLIDA: I probably knew you even less, yet I went with you.

WANGEL: At least you had some idea about the kind of life you were going to. What do you know about him? Nothing. Not even who he is.

ELLIDA: [*staring, unseeing*] That's true. And that's what makes it so dreadful.

WANGEL: Of course it's dreadful.

ELLIDA: That's also why I feel I must do it.

WANGEL: Because you dread it so much?

ELLIDA: Exactly.

WANGEL: [*moving closer*] Ellida, tell me—what do you mean by dreadful?

ELLIDA: [*reflectively*] The dreadful … it both frightens and fascinates. Mostly fascinates.

WANGEL: [*slowly*] You are of the sea.

ELLIDA: That's what's dreadful, too.

WANGEL: It's also what I dread in you. You frighten, and fascinate.

ELLIDA: You feel that?

WANGEL: I'm beginning to realise that I've never known you, not truly known you.

ELLIDA: That's why you must give me my freedom! I'm not what you thought I was. Now you can see that for yourself. Now that we both understand, we can part freely.

WANGEL: [*heavily*] Perhaps it's best for both of us if we part— Still, I can't! For me, you are what I fear. And what fascinates me. That is what gives you your power.

ELLIDA: Do you believe that?

WANGEL: Let's try to get through this day calmly and rationally. I don't dare to release you yet. Not today. I have no right to, Ellida. I have to fulfil my duty and protect you.

ELLIDA: Protect me? What is there to protect me against? There's no brutal external force threatening me. What I dread lies deeper, Wangel! The frightening, fascinating thing lies within myself. What can you do about that?

WANGEL: I can support you, give you strength to resist it.

ELLIDA: But I don't know if I want to resist it!

WANGEL: Tonight everything will be decided, Ellida—

ELLIDA: [*interrupting*] Yes! The turning point of my life.

WANGEL: And tomorrow?

ELLIDA: Perhaps by tomorrow I'll have forfeited my true life.

WANGEL: True life?

ELLIDA: A rich and full life of freedom forfeited. My life and perhaps his too.

WANGEL: [*low voice, grabs her wrist*] Ellida—do you love this man, this stranger?

ELLIDA: All I know is that he fills me with dread, and that—

*She breaks off.*

WANGEL: And that?

ELLIDA: [*tearing herself away*] And that I feel it's with him I belong.

WANGEL: [*bowing his head*] I'm beginning to understand what's at the heart of this.

ELLIDA: So how can you help against it? What advice can you give me?

WANGEL: [*looking at her, heavily*] Tomorrow … he'll have gone. The danger will have lifted. And then I'll be willing to release you and let you go.

ELLIDA: But Wangel, tomorrow will be too late!

WANGEL: [*looking towards the garden*] The children! At least let's spare the children, for as long as we can.

ARNHOLM, BOLETTE, HILDE *and* LYNGSTRAND *come from the garden.* LYNGSTRAND *says his goodbyes and exits, left. The others enter the room.*

ARNHOLM: Well, we've been making some plans—

HILDE: We want to go out on the fjord tonight and—

BOLETTE: No, don't say anything!

WANGEL: We, too, have been making some plans.

ARNHOLM: Ah ... have you?

WANGEL: Tomorrow, Ellida is leaving for Skjoldviken. For a while.

BOLETTE: Leaving us?

ARNHOLM: Very sensible, Mrs Wangel.

WANGEL: Ellida wants to go home again. Home to the ocean.

> HILDE *runs towards* ELLIDA.

HILDE: You're leaving? Leaving us?

ELLIDA: [*dismayed*] Why Hilde, what's the matter?

HILDE: [*pulling herself together*] Oh, it's nothing. [*Half-loud voice as she turns away*] Go on then. Leave, why don't you!

BOLETTE: [*tearful*] Father, you're going too! To Skjoldviken.

WANGEL: Of course I'm not! Perhaps I'll go for a visit now and then—

BOLETTE: And us?

WANGEL: I'll visit you too—

BOLETTE: Now and then! Yes.

WANGEL: My dear child, there's nothing else for it.

> *He walks across the room.*

ARNHOLM: We'll talk about it later, Bolette.

> ARNHOLM *goes to* WANGEL, *they talk quietly together by the door.*

ELLIDA: [*quietly, to* BOLETTE] Why is Hilde so upset?

BOLETTE: Surely you've noticed what Hilde has been longing for, day after day? Ever since you came into this house?

ELLIDA: I didn't realise—

BOLETTE: One single, affectionate word from you.

ELLIDA: Ah. If only I had some room in here ...

> ELLIDA *clasps her hands to her head and stares straight ahead, motionless, as though torn by conflicting thoughts and feelings.* WANGEL *and* ARNHOLM, *whispering, walk across the room, right.* BOLETTE *goes and looks into a side room, right. Then she opens the door wide.*

BOLETTE: The food's on the table.

WANGEL: Good. Mr Arnholm, please! Let's go in and drink a farewell toast to—to 'the woman from the sea'.

*They walk towards the door, right.*

# ACT FIVE

*A secluded corner of Dr Wangel's garden, by the pond. The deepening twilight of a summer night.* ARNHOLM, BOLETTE, LYNGSTRAND *and* HILDE *punt along the bank in a boat, from the left.*

HILDE: We could jump ashore here.

ARNHOLM: No, no, let's not.

LYNGSTRAND: I can't jump, Hilde.

HILDE: Mr Arnholm? Can you jump?

ARNHOLM: I'd prefer not to.

BOLETTE: Let's dock at the steps of Mother's hut, then.

> *They punt out, right. As they do,* BALLESTED *enters along the footpath, right, carrying a French Horn and sheets of music. He waves to them and turns and speaks to them. Their replies become more and more distant.*

BALLESTED: What did you say? Of course, it's because of the English steamer. Well, it's the last time it comes here this year. But if you want to enjoy the music, you'd better not wait much longer. [*Shouting*] What? [*He shakes his head.*] Can't hear what you're saying!

> ELLIDA *and* DR WANGEL *enter left.* ELLIDA *wears a shawl over her head.*

WANGEL: But I assure you, Ellida—there's plenty of time.

ELLIDA: No, no! There isn't! He could come any moment.

BALLESTED: [*on the other side of the fence*] Well well, good evening, Doctor! Good evening, Madam!

WANGEL: Ah, Mr Ballested. Is there going to be music tonight as well?

BALLESTED: Yes. The Horn Association intends to entertain us, I've heard. There's no lack of festive occasions these days. Tonight it's in honour of the English steamer.

ELLIDA: Can you see it already?

BALLESTED: Not yet. But it's coming down the fjord through the islands.

But she'll loom before our eyes before you know it!

ELLIDA: Yes. She will.

WANGEL *partly turns to address* ELLIDA.

WANGEL: Tonight is her last voyage. Then she won't come again.

BALLESTED: A tragic thought, Doctor. Alas, alas! Soon the happy summer time comes to an end. 'Soon all seaward passage shall be closed', as the tragedy laments.

ELLIDA: All seaward passage shall be closed, yes.

BALLESTED: It's hard to reconcile yourself to the dark days ahead. To begin with, I mean. People can alci— a— aclimatise themselves, Mrs Wangel. Indeed they can.

*He bows and goes out, left.*

ELLIDA: [*looking out over the fjord*] Oh this aching suspense! This agonising hour before the moment of decision.

WANGEL: You're still determined to speak with him yourself?

ELLIDA: I have to speak with him. I must make my choice of my own free will.

WANGEL: You have no choice to make, Ellida. I can't allow you to choose.

ELLIDA: You can't stop me from choosing. You can forbid me to leave with him, to follow him, if that's what I choose. You can keep me here by force. Against my will. You have the power to do that. But my choice comes from deep inside me, and whatever I choose there is something you cannot prevent.

WANGEL: You're right. I cannot prevent that.

ELLIDA: I have nothing to resist it with! I have no roots here, Wangel. The children don't belong to me; there's no place for me in their hearts. If I leave tomorrow, whether with him or to Skjoldviken, I don't even have a key to leave behind. No instructions to give about anything, to anyone. I have been on the outside of everything, from the very beginning.

WANGEL: That was the way you wanted it.

ELLIDA: No I didn't. I just simply let things stay the way there were when I arrived. It's you, and no-one else, who wanted it that way.

WANGEL: I wanted what was best for you.

ELLIDA: Oh, I know you did. But there's retribution in this. Revenge. Because now, there's nothing to hold me here, I'm not drawn towards any of the things we should've shared.

WANGEL: I realise that now, Ellida. That's why, from tomorrow, you will have your freedom again. You will be able to live your own life.

ELLIDA: Oh no, my own, my true life lost all sense of direction when I entered yours. [*She clasps her hands in anguish.*] And now he's coming to offer me, for the last and only time, the chance to live my life over again. The life that frightens and fascinates.

WANGEL: That's why you need your husband—and your doctor—to guide you, to act on your behalf.

ELLIDA: Believe me, there are moments when I think how safe and peaceful it would be to take refuge in you. To defy everything that frightens and fascinates me. But I can't do that either. Don't you see?

WANGEL: Come, Ellida, let's walk together.

ELLIDA: I'd like to. But I don't dare. He said I should wait for him here.

WANGEL: Come. There's still plenty of time.

ELLIDA: Is there?

> *They go out, downstage right. As they do,* ARNHOLM *and* BOLETTE *appear by the upper bank of the pond.* BOLETTE *notices them.*

BOLETTE: Look!

ARNHOLM: [*low voice*] Let them go.

BOLETTE: Have you noticed what's been going on between them these last few days?

> ARNHOLM *shrugs his shoulders.*

Of course you have. It's just that you refuse to come out with it.

ARNHOLM: I do think it'd be good for everyone if she got away now and then.

BOLETTE: If she goes to Skjoldviken tomorrow, she'll never come back again.

ARNHOLM: What makes you say that?

BOLETTE: You wait and see! She won't come back. Not as long as Hilde and I are in the house.

ARNHOLM: Both of you?

BOLETTE: Well, perhaps it could work with Hilde. Deep down, I think she adores Ellida. But it's different with me. A stepmother not much older than oneself …

ARNHOLM: Bolette—perhaps it may not be that long before you'll be able to leave yourself.

BOLETTE: [*eagerly*] Really! So you've spoken to father?

ARNHOLM: Well, your father's so preoccupied with other things just now—

BOLETTE: Yes, yes, that's what I said before.

ARNHOLM: But—you mustn't count on any help from him.

BOLETTE: No?

ARNHOLM: He explained his circumstances quite clearly. He felt it was impossible for him to help financially—

BOLETTE: Are you making fun of me?

ARNHOLM: [*continuing*] But it's entirely up to you whether you go away from here or not. You can still see the world. Learn all the things you want to learn. Experience all the things you've been longing to do.

BOLETTE: [*clasping her hands*] But it's impossible, if Father won't help. I have no-one else to turn to.

ARNHOLM: Would you be prepared to accept help from your old—I mean your former teacher?

BOLETTE: From you?

ARNHOLM: Yes. Gladly. You can depend on it. Do you accept?

BOLETTE: To be able to get out, to see the world, to learn something!

   *Pause.*

But how can I possible accept such an offer from a stranger?

ARNHOLM: From me you can accept anything.

BOLETTE: [*seizing his hands*] I don't know why, but—I do believe I can! [*Exclaiming*] Will I really be able to live after all?

ARNHOLM: But please tell me, is there anything at all that binds you here?

BOLETTE: No.

*Pause.*

Except—except for Father, of course. And Hilde.

ARNHOLM: Well, you'll have to leave them sooner or later. And Hilde will go her own way some day. But apart from that, there's nothing? No special relationship?

BOLETTE: None at all. I'm free in that sense.

ARNHOLM: In that case, dear Bolette—you'll travel with me.

BOLETTE: [*clasping her hands*] Oh my God, what a wonderful thought!

ARNHOLM: Well—if you are free, and there's no binding relationship, I would like to ask you if you could—if you would, tie yourself to me? For life.

BOLETTE: [*stepping back*] What?

ARNHOLM: Do you want to be my wife?

BOLETTE: [*half despairing*] No, no no! That's absolutely impossible!

ARNHOLM: Would it really be so impossible for you to—?

BOLETTE: Surely you can't mean what you're saying, Mr Arnholm! [*She looks closely at him*] Or was that what you meant—when you offered me so much?

ARNHOLM: Bolette, listen to me. I'm sorry if I've taken you by surprise. You couldn't know—that it was because of you I came here.

BOLETTE: Because of me?

ARNHOLM: Yes, I'm here because of you. Last spring I had a letter from your father. There was a sentence in it that led me to believe that—that perhaps you thought of your one-time teacher as more than just a friend.

BOLETTE: How could Father write something like that?

ARNHOLM: I misread it. But since then, I have made myself believe that there was a young girl here longing for my return— No, don't interrupt me, please. And such a belief creates a deep impression. It developed into a vivid, a sincere affection for you. I had to come and see you again. Tell you that I shared those feelings I believed you had for me.

BOLETTE: But now that you know it's not like that? That it's a mistake?

ARNHOLM: Makes no difference, Bolette. The image of you that I carry in my heart will always remain coloured by that illusion.

BOLETTE: But Mr Arnholm—you've been my teacher. I can't imagine any other relationship with you.

ARNHOLM: If that's how you feel, then our relationship will remain unchanged. Naturally, I stand by my offer. I'll still help you to get away from here and see the world. I will always be your friend.

BOLETTE: Oh God, Mr Arnholm, it's not possible now. Surely you understand that I cannot accept all that from you now?

ARNHOLM: You would prefer to sit at home and let life pass you by? You want to lose the chance to see the world outside? To take part in all the things you've always longed for?

BOLETTE: Of course not.

ARNHOLM: And when your father's no longer here, to be alone in the world, without help? To have to give yourself to another man, maybe—possibly one you might care for even less?

BOLETTE: Everything you say is true. But even so!—And yet.

ARNHOLM: Yes?

BOLETTE: [*looking doubtfully at him*] Perhaps it's not so impossible after all? Perhaps I might agree to—what you suggested.

ARNHOLM: You mean you'll be willing to let me help you as a friend? Or at least consider it?

BOLETTE: No, no no! That's impossible. No, I would rather you take me as—

ARNHOLM: As my wife?

BOLETTE: Yes. If you still feel that—that's possible—

ARNHOLM: If I still feel—! [*Seizing her hands*] Oh thank you! What you said earlier, your doubts … that doesn't discourage me. I'll find a way to your heart. Oh, Bolette, I'll carry you so carefully!

BOLETTE: I'll get to see the world. To live my life. You've promised me that.

ARNHOLM: And I'll keep that promise.

BOLETTE: And be able to learn anything I want. [*Quietly, immersed in her own thoughts*] Imagine. To be free, to go out into the unknown. And not have to worry about the future.

ARNHOLM: You'll never have to give a thought to that. [*Putting his arm around her waist*] Oh you'll see. We'll be lovely and safe and intimate together, Bolette.

BOLETTE: Yes. It might work. [*Looking out right, and quickly freeing herself*] Shh! Don't say anything yet.

ARNHOLM: What is it?

BOLETTE *points.*

Your father?

BOLETTE: No, the young sculptor. He's walking with Hilde. He's in such frail health.

ARNHOLM: Unless it's just his imagination.

BOLETTE: I believe he won't last long. But perhaps it's for the best.

ARNHOLM: For the best?

BOLETTE: Because of his art. Nothing will come of it, I'm afraid. Let's go before they get here.

HILDE *and* LYNGSTRAND *appear by the pond.*

HILDE: Hi there! M'lord and M'lady! Aren't you going to wait for us?

ARNHOLM: Bolette and I would prefer to be walk for ourselves just now.

ARNHOLM *and* BOLETTE *go out, left.*

LYNGSTRAND: [*laughing*] It's really enjoyable here now. Everyone walking around in couples. Always two by two.

HILDE: [*looking after them*] I bet you anything he's going to propose to her.

LYNGSTRAND: What? But Miss Bolette would never accept him.

HILDE: No. She thinks he's too old. Besides, she told me he's going bald.

LYNGSTRAND: Yes, but that's not the only thing. She'll never have him anyway.

HILDE: How do you know?

LYNGSTRAND: Because she has promised to think about someone else.

HILDE: Only to think about?

LYNGSTRAND: Yes. While he's away.

HILDE: I see. So it's you?

LYNGSTRAND: Yes, imagine that. She promised me! But don't tell her you know.

HILDE: Oh God forbid! And when you come back, will the two of you get engaged? And then married?

LYNGSTRAND: No, that wouldn't work. I couldn't afford to think about things like that for a while. And when I've got myself established—I suppose she'll be a bit too old for me.

HILDE: But you still expect her to stay here and think about you?

LYNGSTRAND: Yes, you see that'd be very useful for me as an artist. And she could easily do it, as she herself has no real vocation in life. Still, it's very sweet of her.

HILDE: So you think you'll get on better with your works of art if you know Bolette is sitting here as a sort of muse?

LYNGSTRAND: Yes, the knowledge that somewhere in the world, a young woman, silent and lovely, is quietly dreaming about you—I think that must be something so ... so ... I don't know how to describe it.

HILDE: Inspiring?

LYNGSTRAND: Yes, that's it. Inspiring. More or less. You're so wise, Miss Hilde. You really are—very wise [*Glances briefly at her*]. When I come home again, you'll be about the same age as your sister is now. Perhaps you'll even look a bit like her. Even have a similar mind. And then you'll have become yourself *and* her—all in one 'gestalt' so to speak.

HILDE: Would you like that?

LYNGSTRAND: I don't really know. Yes, I think I would. But just now, this summer, I prefer you to be yourself. Exactly as you are.

HILDE: You like me best as I am?

LYNGSTRAND: Yes, very much, just as you are.

HILDE: Tell me—as an artist—do you approve of my wearing these light summer clothes?

LYNGSTRAND: I certainly do.

HILDE: Do you think these light colours suit me?

LYNGSTRAND: Yes, lightness suits you beautifully, in my opinion.

HILDE: But tell me then—as an artist—how do you think I'd look in black?

LYNGSTRAND: Black?

HILDE: Yes, all in black. Do you think I'd look good in that?

LYNGSTRAND: Black isn't really for summer. All the same, I'm sure you'd look beautiful in black, too. But yes, with your looks you would.

HILDE: [*looking into space*] Black frills all around, black gloves ... and a long black veil trailing behind.

LYNGSTRAND: If you dressed like that, I'd have wanted to be a painter. I'd have wanted to paint a beautiful young widow in mourning.

HILDE: Or a young bride, in mourning.

LYNGSTRAND: Yes, that would suit you even better. But why would you want to dress like that?

HILDE: I don't really know. But it's an inspiring thought. [*Points, left*] Look! There!

LYNGSTRAND: The big English steamer.

> WANGEL *and* ELLIDA *appear by the pond.*

WANGEL: I assure you, Ellida, you're wrong! [*Seeing the others*] It hasn't come into sight yet, has it, Mr Lyngstrand?

LYNGSTRAND: [*pointing*] There it is already, Dr Wangel.

ELLIDA: I knew it!

LYNGSTRAND: Silently, soundlessly, like a thief in the night.

WANGEL: Take Hilde down to the quay, will you? Hurry! I'm sure she'd love to hear the music.

LYNGSTRAND: We were just going down.

HILDE: [*whispering to* LYNGSTRAND] In pairs.

> HILDE *and* LYNGSTRAND *walk out through the garden, left. The distant brass band music is heard from the fjord.*

ELLIDA: Yes, he is here. I can feel it.

WANGEL: Go inside, Ellida. Let me speak to him alone.

ELLIDA: Oh, it's impossible! Impossible, I told you! [*Crying out*] There—do you see him, Wangel!

> *The* STRANGER *enters, left, and stands on the path outside.*

STRANGER: Good evening. Here you have me again, Ellida.

ELLIDA: Yes. Yes, the hour has come.

STRANGER: Are you ready to leave? Or not?

WANGEL: You can see she's not.

STRANGER: I'm not referring to luggage. Everything she needs is already on board. [*To* ELLIDA] I'm asking if you are ready to come with me; to come with me of your own free will.

ELLIDA: [*imploringly*] Please don't ask me! Don't tempt me!

*The sound of a ship's bell.*

STRANGER: The first bell. You must say yes, or no.

ELLIDA: [*wringing her hands*] Decide! Decide for life! And never be able to change it!

STRANGER: Never. In half an hour it'll be too late.

ELLIDA: [*looking at him shyly, searchingly*] Why are you holding on to me so tightly?

STRANGER: Don't you feel, like I do, that we belong together?

ELLIDA: Because of the promise?

STRANGER: Promises bind no-one, man or woman. I hold on to you because I can do nothing else.

ELLIDA: [*low, trembling voice*] Why didn't you come before?

WANGEL: Ellida!

ELLIDA: [*exclaiming*] What is this ability to fascinate me? Entice me into the unknown! All the power of the ocean …

*The* STRANGER *climbs over the fence.* ELLIDA *hides behind* WANGEL.

STRANGER: I see it. I hear it. Ellida, you will choose me in the end.

WANGEL: [*taking a step towards him*] My wife has no choice in this. It is my duty to choose for her. To guide and guard her. Unless you go away, leave the country, and never come back, you know what you're risking, don't you?

ELLIDA: No, Wangel! Not that!

STRANGER: What would you do to me?

WANGEL: I'll have you arrested. Immediately. I know everything about the murder out there at Skjoldviken.

ELLIDA: Oh Wangel, how could you—!

STRANGER: I was prepared for this.

*He pulls out a revolver.* ELLIDA *throws herself in front of* WANGEL.

ELLIDA: No! No! Don't kill him! Kill me instead.

STRANGER: Not you and not him either. This is for myself. I will live and die a free man.

ELLIDA: [*with mounting agitation*] Listen to me Wangel! I want to tell you this in front of him. Yes, you can keep me here. You have the power and the means to do it. But you have no power over my mind—all my thoughts, my longings and desires! They will search the unknown, yearning for the life I was born to live. A life you have denied me.

WANGEL: [*painfully*] I can see that now, Ellida. You are slipping away from me, little by little. This quest for the boundless and the infinite, for the unattainable, will in the end drive your mind into a deep darkness.

ELLIDA: Oh yes. I can feel it. Like silent black wings hovering over me.

WANGEL: It must never come to that. I see no other means of saving you. And so … I agree to break our deal. From now on, you are free to choose your own path. Completely free to choose.

ELLIDA *stares at him, momentarily speechless.*

ELLIDA: Is it true? Do you mean it, do you really mean it?

WANGEL: Yes, Ellida. I mean it from the depths of my anguished heart.

ELLIDA: But can you do it?

WANGEL: Yes, I can. I can, because I love you so much.

ELLIDA: [*low, trembling voice*] Have I come to mean so much to you?

WANGEL: That's what our years together have done.

ELLIDA: And I … I never saw it.

WANGEL: Your thoughts were elsewhere. But now you're entirely free of me, and all that's mine. Now your life can return to its true path. Now you can choose in freedom. Now it's your responsibility, Ellida, your decision.

ELLIDA: [*clasping her head with her hands, staring at him*] Freedom. And responsibility! That, too!

*The ship's bell sounds again.*

STRANGER: Do you hear, Ellida! It calls for the last time. Come!

ELLIDA: [*turning to look at him intently, firmly*] I can never go with you now.

STRANGER: You're not coming?

ELLIDA: [*clinging to* WANGEL] I can never leave you after this.

WANGEL: Ellida!

STRANGER: All over then?

ELLIDA: Yes. All over. For ever.

STRANGER: I see it now. There is something stronger here than my will.

ELLIDA: Your will has no power over me any longer. To me, you are but a dead man, who has come from the ocean, and returns to it. You no longer fascinate me. And I no longer fear you.

STRANGER: Goodbye, Mrs Wangel. [*He vaults the fence.*] From now on, you are no more than a shipwreck to me. One I survived.

*The* STRANGER *goes out, left.*

WANGEL: [*looking at her for a while*] Ellida, your mind is like the ocean. It ebbs and flows. What caused this wondrous sea change?

ELLIDA: Don't you understand? The change came when I could choose freely.

WANGEL: And the unknown? Does it no longer fascinate you?

ELLIDA: Neither fascinates nor frightens. You allowed me to see into its depths. I could have entered it, had I wanted to. I was free to choose. So I was free to reject it.

WANGEL: I'm beginning to understand you. Your restless longing for the ocean, your fascination for the stranger—these were expressions of a yearning for freedom. Your own freedom, that's all.

ELLIDA: You were a good doctor to me. You dared to use the right medicine.

WANGEL: When things become desperate, a doctor must act daringly. So Ellida, will you come back to me?

ELLIDA: Yes. Now I'll come back to you. Of my own free will, responsible for my own choices.

WANGEL: Ellida! Ellida! From now on we can live for each other.

ELLIDA: And share a past. Yours, as well as mine. And with our two children.

WANGEL: *Our* children?

ELLIDA: I don't own them, but I will win them over.

WANGEL: Our children! [*He kisses her hands*] I can't thank you enough for that word.

> HILDE, BALLESTED, LYNGSTRAND, ARNHOLM *and* BOLETTE *come into the garden, from left, as a number of young townsfolk and summer visitors pass along the footpath.*

HILDE: [*low voice, to* LYNGSTRAND] Ellida and Father look like they've just got engaged.

> BALLESTED *hears* HILDE.

BALLESTED: Ah—summertime, little miss.

ARNHOLM: [*looking at* ELLIDA *and* WANGEL] The Englishman is setting sails.

BOLETTE: [*walking to the fence*] This is the best spot to watch.

LYNGSTRAND: The final voyage of the year.

BALLESTED: 'Soon all seaward passage shall be closed', as the poet says. A sad thought, Mrs Wangel. And now we'll be losing you, too, for a time. You're moving out to Skjoldviken tomorrow, I hear.

WANGEL: No, not anymore. This evening we both changed our minds.

ARNHOLM: [*looking from one to the other*] You did?

BOLETTE: [*moving towards them*] Father—is this really true?

HILDE: [*moving towards* ELLIDA] Are you staying with us after all?

ELLIDA: Yes, Hilde, I am. If you want me.

HILDE: [*struggling between laughter and tears*] If I want you?

ARNHOLM: [*to* ELLIDA] Well, well. This is a surprise.

ELLIDA: [*seriously, while smiling*] You see, Mr Arnholm—we talked about it yesterday, remember? Once you have become a land creature, you can never find a way back to the ocean. Or to ocean life.

BALLESTED: But that's exactly like my mermaid!

ELLIDA: You could say that.

BALLESTED: Except for one thing. The mermaid dies. Humans, on the other hand, can ac— climatise themselves.

ELLIDA: They can, if they're free to do so.

WANGEL: And given responsibility.

ELLIDA: [*giving him her hand*] That's exactly right.

> *The big steamer glides silently out across the fjord.*

> *The music grows louder.*

### THE END

# LA MAMA

presents

# ELLIDA

a new translation by **May-Brit Akerholt**
of **Henrik Ibsen**'s *The Lady from the Sea*

16–27 May 2018

BALLESTED **Dave Evans**
BOLETTE **Meg Spencer**
LYNGSTRAND **Martin Quinn**
HILDE **Esther Myles**
DR WANGEL **Jason Cavanagh**
ARNHOLM **Gabriel Partington**
ELLIDA **Annie Thorold**
THE STRANGER **Frank Handrum**

Director **Laurence Strangio**
Designer **Mattea Davies**
Lighting designer **Georgia Stefania Rann**
Music performed by **Dave Evans**
Dramaturgy **May-Brit Akerholt, Laurence Strangio** and **Annie Thorold**
Assistant Director **Eva Justine Torkkola**

# ⬤ LA MAMA

CEO & Artistic Director
**Liz Jones**

CEO and Manager / Producer
**Caitlin Dullard**

Venue Manager
**Hayley Fox**

Front-of-House Manager
**Amber Hart**

Marketing and Communications
**Sophia Constantine**

Design and Social Media
**Jen Tran**

Office Coordinator
**Elena Larkin**

Learning Producer and School Publications Coordinator
**Maureen Hartley**

Preservation Coordinator
**Fiona Wiseman**

La Mama Musica Curator
**Annabel Warmington**

La Mama Poetica Curator
**Amanda Anastasi**

Script Appraiser
**Graham Downey**

Casting Service
**Zac Kazepis**

Level 1, 205 Faraday Street, Carlton VIC 3053
www.lamama.com.au | info@lamama.com.au
facebook.com/lamama.theatre | twitter.com/lamamatheatre
Office phone 03 9347 6948 | Office Mon–Fri, 10:30am–5:30pm

## FRONT OF HOUSE STAFF

Susan Bamford-Caleo, Carmelina Di Guglielmo, Laurence Strangio, Dennis Coard, Darren Vizer, Robyn Clancy, Zac Kazepis, Aaron Bradbrook, Anna Ellis, Alex Woollatt, Annie Thorold, Helen Doig.

## COMMITTEE OF MANAGEMENT

Sue Broadway, David Levin, Caroline Lee, Dur-é Dara, Richard Watts, Helen Hopkins, Beng Oh, Ben Grant, Liz Jones.

Our sincerest thanks to the many volunteers who generously give their time in support of La Mama.

La Mama's Committee of Management, staff and its wider theatrical community acknowledge that our theatre is on traditional Wurundjeri land.

The La Mama community acknowledges the considerable support it has received in the past decade from Jeanne Pratt and The Pratt Foundation.

La Mama is financially assisted by the Australian Government through the Australia Council—its arts funding and advisory body, the Victorian Government through Creative Victoria—Department of Premier and Cabinet, and the City of Melbourne through the Arts and Culture triennial funding program.

**Australian Government**

Australia | Council
for the Arts

**CREATIVE VICTORIA**

**CITY OF MELBOURNE**

## ACKNOWLEDGEMENTS

Particular acknowledgement and appreciation go to Dr May-Brit Akerholt for her boundless and generous enthusiasm in tackling this translation afresh. Her extensive knowledge, expertise and familiarity with Ibsen and his language have deepened and expanded our understanding of the play immensely and the conversations between the three of us—May-Brit, Annie and myself—have been lively, detailed and stimulating (and multi-lingual!).

To all the staff at La Mama for their invaluable assistance; to Liz Jones and Caitlin Dullard in particular for their neverending patience with the projects that I propose and especially to Maureen Hartley for her constant guidance and support as La Mama Learning Producer.

To the VCAA for programming this work on the 2018 Theatre Studies Playlist and to Helen Champion in particular for being a willing and responsive sounding board to my early less-articulate ideas for this proposal.

To the creative team and cast for trusting in this strange amalgam of Ibsen and Brecht and sacrificing their time and creative energy to the creation of independent theatre on a shoestring budget.

To Annie Thorold for rekindling my interest in this play and for proving to be a true collaborator over this past year, challenging my ideas as well as extending them—and also to be a true *selkie*, as much at home at sea as on the land.

Laurence Strangio

I want to thank Laurence Strangio and Annie Thorold for their passion about this project, and their whole-hearted energy in making it happen. It has been a thoroughly enjoyable process.

May-Brit Akerholt

# A NOTE ABOUT IBSEN AND THE PLAY

*The development of the human race took the wrong path from the beginning. The human children should have evolved as creatures of the sea.*

*– Henrik Ibsen, letter to Count Milewski, Summer 1897*

HENRIK JOHAN IBSEN (March 1828–May 1906) was born into a sea merchant family in Skien, Norway. He wrote his first play *Catiline* in 1850, the year he moved to the capital Christiania (later Oslo). He worked as a dramaturg and director for many years with theatres there as well as in Bergen. In 1864 he and his wife Suzanna Thoresen left Norway to live in Italy, then Germany, where Ibsen wrote his most important plays, including *Peer Gynt, The Pillars of Society, A Doll's House, Ghosts, Hedda Gabler, The Wild Duck, Master Builder, John Gabriel Borkman*. In 1885 he returned to Norway for only the second time in over twenty years, staying for two months at Molde on the Atlantic coast. He spent much time by the sea and later wrote:

*The lure of the sea. Longing for the sea. People's affinity to the sea. Tied to the sea. Dependent on the sea. Compulsion to return to it. … Images of the teeming life of the sea and of 'things lost for ever'. … The sea has power over moods, has its own willpower. The sea can hypnotise.* (June 5, 1888)

Written in Munich in 1888, the play *Ellida (The Lady from the Sea)* is said to be inspired by a couple of legends: that of a creature (Norwegian of Finnish background) whose magically compelling eyes could lure a wife away from her husband; and the story of a sailor who had been away from home for so long that he was thought to be dead, and returned home to find his wife married to another man.

Ibsen's mother-in-law Magdalene Thoresen, who had fled from Denmark to escape from an Icelandic poet, and married a clergyman seventeen years older than herself, wrote:

*While studying in Copenhagen, I met a young man, a wild, strange, elemental creature. We studied together, and I had to yield before his monstrous and demonic will. With him, I could have found passion and fulfillment; I still believe that. ... I met a better person, and have lived a better life, but I have always been conscious that he could have nurtured into flower that love of which my spirit was capable.*

Ibsen returned to live in Norway in 1891. His final play, *When We Dead Awaken,* was written in 1899.


## DIRECTOR'S NOTE

*I shall write no more controversial plays...*

—attributed to Ibsen, 1888


This play both fascinates and frustrates me. Its themes—independence, desire, freedom, responsibility, nature, true partnership—are so relevant and contemporary. Its setting is so infused with Nature—a coastal town, clifftop views, its constant references to the open sea—that it is almost allegorical. Its mysteries—a stranger returned from the past, a sea-bound wedding ceremony, a dead child with mysterious eyes—are so potently symbolic and psychological. Its women are complex and intelligent, each negotiating the confines of society in their own way in their attempts to establish their true identities and free themselves from dependence.

And then there's the ending...

The characters seem happy, there is a renewal of one marriage and the prospect of another and a further muse-like relationship in the wings. Yet the summer is ending, the ship has sailed and the ice is closing in—the imagery could not be more blatant nor more bleak. Is Ibsen avoiding controversy or hinting at darker times ahead? Is this the longed-for ideal marriage or the compromise of safety and convention? There is clearly an ambiguity intended here, not the simple 'happy ending' that it appears to be.

The choices on offer—particularly for Ellida and Bolette—are presented as absolute contrasts: either one bond or another, no possibility for true independence. Even Hilde's fascination with Lyngstrand is unhealthily perverse. The women's power to choose is continually compromised by the limitations of choice presented to them—both in their relationships with men and their relationships with each other. Seen in this way, the world of *Ellida* is one of binaries—land/sea, freedom/responsibility, marriage/independence—a closed world that does not allow for 'free will' and individual determination nor really for true cooperation, but demands renunciation and submission.

In order to counter this oppositional situation, the approach in presenting this play—with all its fraught decisions and manipulative compromises—has been to adopt a Brechtian-inspired critically conscious perspective on these 'moments of choice'; to be hyper-aware of the limitations of choice available and to present them as such; to offer a counter-staging—within the world of the play—that exposes the gendered power structures that inhibit the women's autonomy and freedom. [Please see the **Production Notes** for more on this.]

Why, when it becomes possible, doesn't Ellida choose her own personal freedom, bound to neither man…? Why does Bolette choose loveless marriage over striking out on her own…? As in other Ibsen plays, financial security undercuts female self-sufficiency. In such circumstances, which of us would have the courage to dive into the unknown ourselves…?

# MAY-BRIT AKERHOLT
## TRANSLATOR/ DRAMATURG

**Dr May-Brit Akerholt** has extensive experience as translator and production dramaturg of classic and contemporary plays. More than 20 of her translations have been produced by leading theatre companies around Australia and overseas. Her published translations include several plays by Ibsen and Strindberg; by Jon Fosse: four volumes of plays (Oberon Books, London); two novels: *The Boathouse*; *Trilogy*; and *Essays* (all by Dalkey Archive Press: UK, US and Ireland). She has written a book on Patrick White's drama and a number of her critical articles have been published in various books and journals. *Ibsen on Theatre* (edited by Frode Helland and Julie Holledge) with new translations of Henrik Ibsen's writings by May-Brit Akerholt is due for publication by Nick Hern Books (London) in 2018.

Positions include: Tutor in the School of English and Linguistics at Macquarie University; Lecturer in Drama at the National Institute of Dramatic Art (NIDA); Resident Dramaturg at Sydney Theatre Company; Artistic Director of the Australian National Playwrights' Centre and the National Playwrights' Conference. Her PhD thesis from the University of Sydney is titled *The Dramaturgy of Translation*.

## LAURENCE STRANGIO
### DIRECTOR / DRAMATURG

**Laurence** is an independent director, dramaturg, theatre-maker and stage-adaptor. Recent productions include *Duras: Desire & Destruction—The Lover + Destroy, She Said* (2018) and *alias Grace, Hotel Bonegilla* and *Beckett: Not I + Eh Joe* (all for La Mama 50th Birthday Festival, 2017). He has produced over 30 works at La Mama including *L'amante anglaise, La Medea, The good person of Szechwan, …waiting for Godot* and *Six characters in search of an author…* He has also directed for Melbourne Festival, Malthouse Theatre, Red Stitch, fortyfivedownstairs, Castlemaine State Festival and Instant Café Theatre (Kuala Lumpur). Laurence has received Green Room Awards for his direction of *Portrait of [Dora]* and *Six characters in search of an author…*

## MATTEA DAVIES
### DESIGNER

**Mattea** is a designer, scenic artist, prop maker, florist, and general purveyor of creative nonsense. She has rarely designed theatre over the last few years but returns to the craft every so often to work with Laurence (being a great believer in quality over quantity). Previous collaborations include *Duras: Desire & Destruction—The Lover + Destroy, She Said* (La Mama Courthouse 2018), *Beckett: Not I + Eh Joe* (La Mama 50th Birthday Festival, 2017), *Nought Point Five Above Zero, No Wind* (La Mama, 2016), *A Kind of Fabulous Hatred* (fortyfivedownstairs, 2013), *The Woods* (La Mama, 2012) and *Uncle Vanya* (fortyfivedownstairs, 2012).

## GEORGIA STEFANIA RANN
### LIGHTING DESIGNER

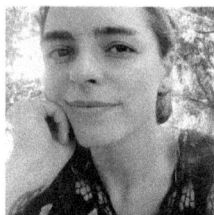

**Georgia** actively collaborates as a spatial designer for theatre and live performance. Her lighting and stage credits include Fairly Lucid's productions *Raton Laveur*, *The Reckoning*, *Member*; Travis Cotton's *Robots Vs Art*; Chamber Made Opera's *The Minotaur Trilogy* and *Opera For A Small Mammal*; and Cynthia Troupe's *Undercoat: A Parafoxical Tale*. More recently Laurence Strangio's productions of *Hotel Bonegilla* and *The Yellow Wallpaper*; and Well sensored *food's black gloves & flowers*.

## EVA JUSTINE TORKKOLA
### ASSISTANT DIRECTOR

**Eva Justine Torkkola** is an Acting Tutor for NIDA Open and studying her Masters of Film and Television at VCA. She has performed in over thirty stage productions including *Hotel Bonegilla* by Tes Lyssiotis (dir. Laurence Strangio), *Wagner in Paris* by Karen Van Spall, *In Wired Rain* by Joachim Matschoss, as well as most recently assistant directing *The Cocoon* by Kotryna Gesait, *Lonely People are Always up in the Middle of the Night* by Hila Ben Gera, *And Then the Snow Fell on Egypt* by Gavin Roach (dir: Sarah Vickery). She is currently writing and directing her own films.

## ANNIE THOROLD
### DRAMATURG / ELLIDA

**Annie Thorold** is a Swedish actor who delights in physical theatre, devised work such as *Killjoy* (Imprint Theatre Co), as well as alternative approaches to classical texts such as *The Yellow Wallpaper* (La Mama Explorations, 2017). Annie has a Bachelor of Performance, Dramatic Arts from the Australian Institute of Music in Sydney. She completed her degree playing the title role in *Anna Karenina* (2016, dir. Peta Downes) and with an internship at La Mama Theatre Melbourne as a dramaturgical associate and performer in the Explorations season of *The Lover*. 2018 productions include the short film *Nature* (by Elizabeth Fermanis) and *Duras: The Lover + Destroy, She Said* (dir. Laurence Strangio, La Mama Courthouse).

## JASON CAVANAGH
### DR WANGEL

**Jason Cavanagh** has been performing for stage and screen since 1998 when he completed a scholarship at St Martins Theatre. In 2002 He graduated from the National Theatre and since then has performed in around 40 stage productions in Melbourne and London. In 2009 he founded The Owl and the Pussycat Theatre in Richmond, which he owned and ran until 2014. He is also the co-founder of 5pound theatre. In 2017 he performed in his fifth season of an award nominated production *Purgatorio* as part of an artist residency program at The Freezer Cultural Centre in Iceland. Currently he is studying Fine Art at RMIT.

## DAVE EVANS
## BALLESTED / MUSICIAN

**Dave** grew up in northeast Victoria. He's played accordion professionally for more than twenty-five years and is a founding member of The Band Who Knew Too Much. He performed a live score for the Australian silent film *The Sentimental Bloke* with Jen Anderson and Dan Warner worldwide. He played Second Songman in the Australian production of the UK National Theatre's *Warhorse*, was accordionist for The Collective's production of *Parade* at fortyfiveownstairs, Black Hole Theatre's *Where The Wild Things Sing*, Colleen Burke's *Death at Intervals* and *Hotel Bonegilla* (both at La Mama). Dave is in quite a few bands and can even occasionally be heard busking in the city.

## FRANK HANDRUM
## THE STRANGER

**Frank Handrum** is a Melbourne-based stage and screen actor born and bred in Norway. He has been in Australia for the last 18 years, and is chuffed to bits to finally appear in a Norwegian play. Frank is also delighted to return to La Mama Courthouse, where he last performed in the play *Cogito* in 2012. Other performance credits include *The Importance of being Ernest*, *25 & F\*cked*, *Dead Technology Memoirs*, *Mystery Radio Theatre*, *The Incredibly Satisfying Adventures of Milton McAffrey P.I.* and *Diabolical* (Winner: Outstanding Male Performance Short+Sweet 2013). He was also once naked on *Neighbours* but won no awards for this performance.

## ESTHER MYLES
### HILDE

**Esther** graduated with a Bachelor of Arts at La Trobe University, double majoring in Literature and Theatre and Drama. While studying Esther performed in numerous student plays at La Trobe and with Melbourne University. She has trained at 16th St Actors Studio as well as completed the full time acting course at Howard Fine Acting Studio in 2017. Esther has worked with independent theatre companies such as RN Productions and Four Letter Word Theatre and performed in productions including Joshua Harmon's *Bad Jews* and Michael Gow's *Live Acts On Stage*. She recently starred in the Melbourne Fringe Festival production *This Is She*.

## GABRIEL PARTINGTON
### ARNHOLM

A graduate of the VCA, **Gabriel** is a Melbourne-based performer with a love for storytelling and cooked breakfasts. Graduating in 2009, Gabriel worked with companies such as Complete Works, Four Larks, OpticNerve, Attic Arctic, 15 Minutes from Anywhere and has collaborated with Laurence Strangio on several projects including the award winning production of Luigi Pirandello's *Six characters in search of an author…* He is a core member of the experimental arts group The Indirect Object, having created with them in Prague, Taiwan and Australia-wide. Gabriel's screen work includes various short films, a silly dairy commercial and roles on *McLeod's Daughters*, *Neighbours* and *Ricketts Lane*.

## MARTIN QUINN
## LYNGSTRAND

**Martin Quinn** is a Sydney-based actor who loves working on new work and devised pieces of theatre. He recently appeared in *Unknowing* at the Blood Moon theatre in Kings Cross and last year in Don't Look Away's production of *Frankenstein* at Theatre Works in St. Kilda. In the future Martin hopes to continue creating original work with an emphasis on physical movement and music. For the present, he is incredibly excited to be working on a May-Brit Akerholt's adaptation and indulging in the wonders of a Melbourne Autumn.

## MEG SPENCER
## BOLETTE

**Meg** is an actor, script-writer, theatre- and film creator. Her stage credits include *Three Sisters, Cloudstreet, A Pillar of Salt, Fallen Angels, Shadows of Angels, Eight, Proctor What, Hell Hath No Fury, Oscar Wilde's Women* and *Tchekov at the House of Special Purpose*. On screen: ABC's *It's A Date, Womb, Cat Sick Blues, Cars with Guns, Aunty Donna Saving a Hot Girl, A Minus* and self-written *Things Are Really Great Here*. She was the recipient of the BAF Nicholson Grant for the Melbourne production of her play *Glasshouse*. Her play *Sufferance* debuted as the opening show for the Melbourne Meat Market's new venue The Stables.

# PRODUCTION NOTES
## Approach to Performance Style

Brecht has been a key inspiration in our approach to this work. Ibsen and Brecht seem to stand at opposite ends of the theatrical spectrum, however Ibsen's plays are primarily social commentary and Brecht's 'theatre of showing' is an ideal method to examine and critique the socially determined contradictions in behaviour presented by the characters. This play filled with choices, contrasts and contradictions demands more than a romanticised 'naturalist' performance style to present its deeper questions and meanings.

Brecht's 'realism' is based on investigating people's behaviours and opinions and recognising that any one person has more than one way of behaving in any given situation. There is an emphasis on *how* things happen and in applying this to a 'naturalistic' play there is a deliberate and conscious presentation of actions and intentions—one that underscores and contrasts the characters' decisions and the social structures at play.

A Brechtian approach also allows us to employ different theatrical devices—direct address, non-illusionistic stagecraft, use of live music, presentational gestures and attitudes—to comment on and underscore the action and significance of the scene. The performers behave as an ensemble as well as individual characters; simple gestures become significant through repetition; the audience is constantly aware that the situation is being presented to them, not merely happening—nothing is inevitable, everything is the result of intentions and decisions.


## Use of Space and Design Elements

The key element of the play is the sea—its vastness, its unknown-ness, its remoteness, its influence. The production uses space, sound, lighting and language to evoke these qualities in non-naturalistic ways. The performance is designed around the concept of minimal furniture and props—this is a world of dreams and imaginings, of things that appear and return. It is also a voyeuristic world where people keep watch on others and are aware of being overheard or observed themselves. The sea is beyond—visible only to the characters, from cliff-top heights and within themselves. It is late summer and the Northern light is glancing and deceptive. And the sound of the sea is ever-present, in reality and in people's minds.

## Use of Language

Ellida and the Stranger share a connection through the sea. In Act 2 Ellida describes their conversations when they used to meet by the lighthouse—*"About storms and calms. Dark nights on the ocean. And the sea sparkling in the sunshine."* This shared sea-sensibility is made tangible in this production through the use of Scandinavian language in the scenes between Ellida and the Stranger. This is not merely a romantic nod to the origins of the play but rather a concrete theatrical representation of the innate potency of that connection and of its seductive power as well. Language is both a connecting force and a weapon of manipulation.

## Use of Music

Music is a subtle but key element in the play—Ballested is the town bandmaster, welcoming and farewelling its visitors, and is in many ways the play's 'Master of Ceremonies'. In this production the performer playing Ballested underscores the performance, providing a steady and subtle musical commentary and emotional counterpoint to the action and themes of the play. Drawing on Scandinavian folk melodies, various thematic elements—the sea, the Stranger, the supernatural—and particular behaviours—possession, coercion, indecision—are represented musically and performed live as direct counterpoint to the action of the characters onstage.

# STANDING OVATION FOR
# AUSTRALIA'S HOME OF INDEPENDENT THEATRE

In 2018 La Mama will celebrate 51 years of nurturing new Australian theatre.

Built in 1883 for Anthony Reuben Ford, a Carlton printer, the building at 205 Faraday Street had been used as a workshop, a boot and shoe factory, an electrical engineering workshop and a silk underwear factory before becoming a theatre in 1967. La Mama was established by Betty Burstall and modelled on experimental theatre activities at La MaMa E.T.C., New York. Jack Hibberd's play *Three Old Friends* was the first play performed in the tiny space.

Since that time the crowded intimacy of La Mama has provided welcome opportunities to a host of playwrights, actors, directors, technicians, film-makers, poets and comedians, such as David Williamson, Barry Dickins, John Romeril, Tes Lyssiotis, Lloyd Jones, Arthur and Corinne Cantrill, Judith Lucy, Richard Frankland, Julia Zemiro, and Cate Blanchett... the list of those who have been nurtured there is long.

Under the capable care of Liz Jones (Artistic Director since 1976), and her La Mama team, more than 50 productions are now produced annually at La Mama, and at our second performance venue, the refurbished La Mama Courthouse, 349 Drummond Street. An ever-increasing audience is drawn not only from the Carlton and Melbourne University environs, but from far and wide across the country.

'I set La Mama up, as a space for writers and directors to perform in but also it was a space where people came, as audience, to participate in the creative experiment.'

—Betty Burstall, Artistic Director of La Mama 1967–76

'Much will be said of La Mama's role in developing a new generation of Australian writing. However, in considering policies and personalities, one should not forget the nature of the space and its impact in making possible performances that would be lost in a large theatre. It gave performances the intimacy of the cinema close-up with the exciting immediacy of the live theatre and the warmth of the coffee lounge.'

—Daryl Wilkinson, Director

La Mama Theatre—which, on various occasions, has been called headquarters, the source, the shopfront and the birthplace of Australian theatre—was classified by the National Trust in 1999.

'The two-storey brick building is of State cultural significance because it has been occupied by La Mama Theatre… The building is indelibly associated with the performance arts and is a rare manifestation of an experimental theatre in Australia…'

—National Trust Classification Report

'When it comes to grassroots Melbourne theatre, La Mama in Carlton is like the 60GB iPod—small, subtle, but containing a whole lot more than you might expect.'

—John Bailey, Age

La Mama produces work from two venues: 205 Faraday Street, Carlton (opposite top), and at the La Mama Courthouse, 349 Drummond Street, Carlton.

For current La Mama productions and events, see www.lamama.com.au.

www.ingramcontent.com/pod-product-compliance
Lightning Source LLC
Chambersburg PA
CBHW040054100426
42734CB00044B/3306